The Gospel of Luke

Translated by
Kalmia Bittleston

Floris Books

First published by Floris Books in 1990

British Library CIP Data available

Phototypeset by Input Typesetting Ltd, London
Printed in Great Britain
by Dotesios Ltd, Trowbridge, Wilts.

Contents

Introduction

The New Testament gives a particularly clear picture of Luke, writer both of the Gospel and its sequel the Acts of the Apostles.

He accompanied Paul on some of his great journeys and voyages, and was his friend and physician as well as his disciple. He learned from Paul, profoundly, and he was recognized from the earliest times as writing in the spirit of Paul's teaching, although there is a marked difference of mood.

In his letters Paul is vigorous and often choleric; Luke shows, in general, a mood of gentleness and restraint, even where severe criticism of the words and actions of the people he is describing is implied.

In the Middle Ages, Luke was sometimes represented as a painter, at work on a portrait of the Mother of Jesus. He may well have learned, before writing his Gospel, from personal meetings at Ephesus with Mary and the beloved disciple, John the Evangelist, as well as earlier from Paul. Luke's writings are indeed different in style from the works attributed to John: the Fourth Gospel, the three Epistles, and the Revelation which ends the New Testament — which are also very different from each other.

It is generally assumed that Luke wrote *before* any of these came into being, and before the fiercest times of persecution of the Christians by the Romans.

For all the Evangelists, and for Paul, the central fact

of which they write is the Resurrection of Christ. But it is characteristic of Luke that he alone describes in detail (14:13–35), among the events of the first Easter Sunday, a *journey*, though not a very long one — the walk of Emmaus, on which two disciples, not members of the twelve are joined by a stranger, whom they do not recognize as Christ, until at supper, he vanishes from their sight. And, although all four Gospels make it clear that during the seven weeks between Easter and Pentecost the Apostles were given their mission to bring their witness to the Resurrection to all peoples, it is Luke who has the most remarkable phrase to describe the greatness of these journeys. The Apostles are to be witness up to the *'eschátou tēs gēs'* (Acts 1:8). *Eschatos* describes what comes *last* in time (as in eschatology) or in space. They are to go to where the world ends. Luke is very much aware that when we truly go on a journey, we change not only our position in space, but our relation to time. We go to meet the future. It is described in Matthew, Mark and John that during the years between the Baptism and the Crucifixion, Christ alternated between Galilee, where many people lived still in something of a dreamlike consciousness, a heritage from the past, and Judea, where men's minds — in fear or hope — were more strongly turned to the future. But much of Luke is occupied with the journey of Christ from Galilee to Jerusalem through Samaria. a last great journey which leads to the Cross and the Resurrection.

Luke is very much aware that these events are the beginning of a great new journey to be undertaken by humanity as a whole, led by Christ Jesus; for only in Luke's Gospel is it said that on the mountain of the Transfiguration the spiritual forms of Moses and Elijah speak with Christ Jesus about his 'going forth' — for this is the literal meaning of the Greek word *exodus* — to be accomplished from Jerusalem, as Moses led out the Israelites on the long journey to the Promised Land (Luke 9:31).

But the counterpart of a journey leading upwards is a journey down which has preceded it. And two of the parables told only in Luke's Gospel, *The Good Samaritan* and *The Prodigal Son*, contain pictures of such downward journeys (10:25–37, 15:11–32).

These stories have had immeasurable moral influence upon human beings, taken quite simply, but they can also be taken as parables of the fate of humanity after the Fall from Paradise, of which Luke is naturally also very much aware. Mankind, going downwards, fell among thieves, was stripped of the robes which expressed his spiritual dignity, beaten, and left half dead. Luke, like Paul, has no doubt at all about the existence of mighty spiritual beings who tempt and rob mankind. This has befallen us; it was not simply our own choice. And yet, from another aspect, humanity has gone willingly on the downward journey, and has been prepared to waste the heritage given from above. We have as a kind of adventure taken the path which leads eventually to hunger and the swine. In the New Testament, swine are a picture of materialism, of a condition of soul in which it is greedily attached to physical things as objects themselves, and not as revelations of the beings who have created them.

It is in the Gospels of Matthew and Luke that an abundance of parables, in the form of detailed stories, can be found. Mark has very few parables; John, in this sense, none at all. Comparing Matthew and Luke, it is directly apparent that the parables told in Luke are rich in mercy and forgiveness while those of Matthew have often a mood of severity and judgment.

But both evangelists indicate that the Parables have, for the disciples, the character of *riddles*. They cannot be taken, *by them*, simply as moral teaching. They challenge them to think actively about their meaning, and above all, about their relation to the Deed of Christ. So it is to be expected that somewhere in each parable, though perhaps deeply hidden, the being of Christ himself is to be found.

For example — who is the Good Samaritan? Some of the medieval artists gave a remarkable answer to this question. They painted the Good Samaritan with the halo containing the red cross about his head, the halo with which Christ himself is painted, particularly after the Resurrection; but also, as by Fra Angelico, the Christ as child. The stranger who comes to the aid of the man who fell among thieves is a bearer of the spirit of Christ — and truly a neighbour.

In the ancient world, for the great majority of mankind, 'neighbours' were people who spent their lives nearby, with similar racial characteristics and with shared traditions and customs inherited from the past. But through the centuries up to the present, the trend has been for more and more people in a great part of the world to have increasingly significant encounters with others whose inherited qualities and customs are different from their own. Love, and healing, and wisdom come to us from strangers, people encountered on journeys. In Luke, this is described in the teaching given by Jesus in the synagogue at Bethlehem, which ends with the words: 'And there were many lepers in

Israel when Elisha was a prophet, but not one of them was cleansed except Naaman, the Syrian'.

This teaching arouses so bitter an anger in the hearers that they have the intention of killing Jesus (Luke 4:29). Some of those who heard the story of the Good Samaritan may well have felt a similar anger; it is the stranger who is the true neighbour.

An encounter on a journey may well prove to be among the most important in the lives of one or both of the participants. Luke gives a striking example in the Acts, with the meeting of Philip the Deacon, and the Ethiopian Minister, who is actually going along in his chariot at the time. An encounter which leads to the Minister's baptism (Acts 8:26).

The story of the Good Samaritan is told in the context of a question about eternal life. To recognize in the stranger the true neighbour and treat him accordingly, may prove, together with the great fourfold love of God (with all your heart, and with all your soul, and with all your strength, and with all your mind), the gateway to eternity in the midst of transitory existence. (Far away, this was expressed in the Zen story *The Gates of Heaven and Hell*.) Humanity as a whole is on a journey and on its way it has encountered robbers. For humanity, as a whole, the Christ is the great stranger met on the way; a stranger coming into earthly existence from the realms of eternity, fully known only by the Father who sent him.

In a passage in which Luke's words (10:22) very much resemble passages from the later chapters of John, Jesus says:

All things
Were handed over to me

By my Father
And no-one understands
Who the Son is
Except the Father
And who the Father is
Except the Son
And those to whom
It is the will of the Son
To reveal him.

In all the Gospel parables, every detail is significant, so we can ask why the Good Samaritan speaks of his return to the inn later? Would not the story have been complete without this? But if we try to enter into the human experience of the man who fell in with robbers, this detail becomes significant. When the Good Samaritan continues on his journey, the injured man is hardly conscious of what has happened to him, or who has helped him. But when the Samaritan returns, they will meet in full consciousness. 'To return' has a deep meaning for Luke. It is he who records one of the most specific statements about the 'Second Coming' of the Christ. At the Ascension, the two men in white robes who appear to the assembly of disciples on the Mount of Olives say: 'This Jesus, who was taken up from you into heaven, will come in the same way as you saw him go into heaven.' (Acts 1:11).

When does Jesus return, and reveal himself to the full consciousness of mankind? In Matthew, Mark and Luke, we find accounts of the Sermon on the Mount of Olives, given to a small number of disciples not long before the Passion. They all (with slight variations in detail) describe a time of great trouble for mankind, in which it is not difficult to recognize many characteristics of the present age (Matt.24 and 25; Mark 13; Luke 21). And in this time, the whole of mankind — not only traditional Christians — is challenged to find a conscious relationship to the Christ: each single individual, wherever he may have been brought up among the varied faiths and world-conceptions of the present.

As it is said in the Apocalypse of John (3:20):
'Behold, I stand at the door and knock.'

Quite particularly, the time of trouble brings distress to mothers of small children (Matt.24:10, Mark 13:17, Luke 21:23):

Alas for the woman
In those days
With a child in her womb
Or one at her breast.

In our day, civilization over a great part of the world has taken shape which is harmful to children. And countless women are torn between the claims of a household with one or more small children, and the task of keeping up with a professional or similar career.

In many old pictures of the Mother of Jesus, one hand is given to her child, and the other holds a book. It is clearly meant that this is a holy book, and a source of wisdom and a giver of strength for the inner life.

A book can only do these things for its readers if it is brought to life. The Greek word for reading, *anagnōsis*, in Greek, is very close to the word for resurrection, *anastasis*. The letter kills; if words are taken only into the head, they are inert: they can be brought to life only in the heart, with ever renewed discovery of their meaning. Then they awaken us, and prepare us to meet the Christ — in the conscious understanding of his deed — through the grace of God.

The Gospels, themselves, are such books. For this reason there is such a longing in our time for renewed understanding of the Gospels and the Bible as a whole, and all the ancient holy books: and for a renewed sense of the presence and work of the Holy Spirit.

May this new translation of Luke do its part in meeting these needs.

Adam Bittleston

The birth, Baptism, and Temptation

Healings and teachings in Galilee

The journey to Jerusalem

1 *Prologue*

1 Since many have taken in hand
 To set down an account
 Of all those events
 Which certainly took place among us

2 As they were committed to us
 By those who from the beginning
 Were themselves able to see
 And to become ministers of the word

3 It seemed good to me also
 Having been able to follow all things
 From their outset
 To write an orderly account for you
 Most excellent Theophilus

4 So that you could be aware
 Of the accuracy of the teaching
 In which you have been instructed

The Angel comes to Zechariah

5 It so happened
 That during the reign of Herod
 King of Judea
 That there was a certain priest
 Belonging to the group of Abijah
 Whose name was Zechariah

 His wife was descended from Aaron
 And she was called Elizabeth

6 They were both upright people
 In the sight of God

Not failing to keep all the commandments
And regulations of the Lord
7 But they had no children
Because Elizabeth was barren
And they were both advanced in age

8 Then it happened
That he was acting as priest before God
In his order of service
9 And according to the custom of priesthood
It fell to him by lot
To enter the shrine of the Lord
And burn incense
10 While all the many people
Were praying outside
At the hour of the censing

11 An angel of the Lord
Appeared to him
Standing on the right side
Of the altar of incense

12 When he saw this
Zechariah was disturbed
And fear fell upon him

13 But the angel said to him
Do not be afraid
Zechariah
Because your request has been heard
Your wife Elizabeth

Will bear you a son
And you shall give him the name
John

14   You will have joy
And great happiness
And many will rejoice
At his birth
15   As he will be great
In the sight of the Lord

He shall not drink any wine
Or strong drink
He will be filled
With the Holy Spirit
Even from his mother's womb
16   And will turn many
Of the sons of Israel
To the Lord their God

17   He will go forth in his sight
In the spirit and power of Elijah
To turn the father's hearts
To the children
And the rebellious
To an understanding of what is right
Preparing for the Lord
A people who are ready for him

18   Zechariah said to the angel
How shall I become aware of this

As I myself am an old man
And my wife is advanced in age

19   The angel answered him
            I
            I am Gabriel
            Who stand in the presence of God
            I was sent out to speak to you
            And to bring you this good news

20   But see
            Now you will be silenced
            And not have the power to speak
            Until this happens
            Because you did not believe
            My words
            Which will be fulfilled
            In their season

21   The people were expecting Zechariah
        And they were astonished
        That he delayed in the shrine

22   When he came out
        He had not the power to speak
        And they became aware
        That he had seen a vision
        In the shrine
        As he signed to them
        And remained dumb

23 And when his term of service
   Came to an end
   He went back to his home

24 After this
   His wife Elizabeth conceived
   And hid herself for five months
       Saying
25   This is what the Lord
              Has done for me
              When he looked upon me
              To take away my disgrace
              Among the people

   The Angel Gabriel comes to Mary
26 Now in the sixth month
   The angel Gabriel
   Was sent out from God
   To a town in Galilee
   Which was called Nazareth

27 To a virgin
   Promised in marriage
   To a man whose name was Joseph
   Belonging to the house of David
   And the virgin's name
   Was Mary

28 When he came to her
       He said

Rejoice
You have been shown favour
The Lord is with you

29　She was much troubled
By what he said
And considered
What sort of greeting
This could be

30　　And the angel said to her
Do not be afraid
Mary
Because you have found favour
With God
31　And see
You will conceive
And bear a son
To whom you should give the name
Jesus

32　　He will be great
And will be called
The Son of the Most High
And the Lord God
Will give him the throne
Of his father David

33　　And he will reign
Over the house of Jacob
Throughout the ages

And his Kingdom
Will have no end

34 Mary said to the angel
How will this come about
As I have no knowledge of man?

35 The angel answered her
The Holy Spirit will come upon you
And the power of the Highest
Will overshadow you
Therefore
The child who will be born
Will be called holy
Son of God

36 And see
Your cousin Elizabeth
Has also conceived a son
In her old age
And this is her sixth month
Although she was considered barren

37 Because nothing which he says
Will be impossible for God

38 Mary replied
See here
The servant of the Lord
Let it happen to me
As you have said

And the angel
Went away from her

Mary visits her cousin Elizabeth
39 In those days
Mary set out
And hurried into the hill country
To a town in Judea
40 Where she entered Zechariah's house
And greeted Elizabeth
41 And so it happened
That when Elizabeth
Heard Mary's greeting
The unborn babe leaped in her womb

Elizabeth was filled with the Holy Spirit
42   And she called out
    With a loud cry
        Blessing on you among women
        And blessing
        On the fruit of your womb
43   What does this mean for me
        That the mother of my Lord
        Has come to me?
44   As indeed
        When the sound of your greeting
        Came to my ears
        The babe in my womb
        Leaped for joy

45 She is blessed
Who has believed
That what the Lord
Has said to her
Will be fulfilled

46 And Mary said
My living soul
Gives high praise to the Lord
47 And my spirit
Rejoiced in God my saviour
48 Because he has looked upon
His servant's humility

See how from this time
All generations will call me blessed
49 Because the Mighty One
Has done great things for me
And holy is his name

50 He is merciful
To those who fear him
From generation to generation

51 He acted
With the strength of his arm
He scattered the proud people
Their hearts' desires came to nothing

52   He brought down the powerful
       From their thrones
       And raised up the humble

53   Those who were hungry
       He filled with good things
       Those who were rich
       He sent away empty

54   He gave help to his servant Israel
       Remembering mercy
       As he had said to our fathers
       To Abraham
       And to his descendants
       Until the ending of the age

56   Mary remained with her
       For about three months
       Then returned to her home

The birth of John the Baptist
57   When Elizabeth's time was fulfilled
       She bore a son

58   Then her neighbours
       And her family
       On hearing that the Lord
       Had shown her great mercy
       Rejoiced with her

59 On the eighth day
They came to circumcise the child
And would have given him the name
Zechariah
After his father

60 But his mother said
No
He must be called John

61 And they said to her
No one in your family
Has been given this name

62 They made signs to the father
As to what name
He wished him to have

63 He asked for a writing tablet
And wrote
His name is John

And they were all astonished

64 Instantly
His mouth was opened
And when his tongue was set free
He spoke in praise of God

65 Fear came upon all the neighbourhood
And these things were discussed
In the hill country of Judea

66 All those who heard of them
Kept them in their hearts
    And said
        What will become of this child?

67 As indeed
The hand of the Lord
Was with him

68 His father Zechariah
Was filled with the Holy Spirit
    And he prophesied
    Saying
        Blessing on the Lord God of Israel
        Because he has come to his people
        And he has obtained their release
69   Raising for us
        A powerful saviour
        From the house of his servant David
70   As he told us
        Through the mouth
        Of his holy prophets of old
71   That we should be saved
        From our enemies
        And out of the hands
        Of all who hate us

72   This mercy
          He granted to our forefathers
          In remembrance of his holy covenant
73   And the oath
          Which he swore to our father
          Abraham
          That he would give us

74   As we have been delivered
          Out of the hands of our enemies
          We may serve him without fear
75   With piety and justice in his sight
          All our days

76   And you child
          Will also be called
          A prophet of the Most High
          As you will go before the Lord
          To make ready his road
77   Bringing knowledge of salvation
          To his people
          In forgiving their sins

78   Because of the compassionate mercy
          Of our God
          Whereby the sun
          Which rises in high heaven
          Will visit us
79   Appearing
          To those who sit in darkness
          And in the shadow of death

To guide our feet
On to a road of peace

80 The child grew
And became strong in spirit

He was in the desert
Until those days
When he appeared openly
Among the people of Israel

2 *The birth of Jesus in Bethlehem*
1 Now it happened in those days
That a decree
Went out from Caesar Augustus
That all those living in the land
Should be registered

2 This first registration
Was made when Quirinius
Governed Syria
3 And all the people
Went to be registered
Every one to his own city

4 Therefore Joseph
Also went up out of Galilee
From the town of Nazareth
To Judea
To the city of David

Which is called Bethlehem
Because he belonged
To the house and family of David

5 To be registered with Mary
His promised bride
Who was with child

6 Now it so happened
That while they were there
The number of her days was completed
7 And she gave birth
To her first born son

She wrapped him in linen bands
And laid him in a manger
Because there was no room for them
In the inn

8 In that region there were shepherds
Who remained out in the fields
Guarding their flock during the night

9 And an angel of the Lord
Came upon them
And the glory of the Lord
Shone around them
And they were shaken with fear

10 The angel said to them
Do not be afraid

See how I bring you
News of great joy
Which will come to all the people

11 Today
In the city of David
A saviour has been born to you
Who is Christ the Lord

12 And this will be a sign
For you
You will find a new born babe
Wrapped in linen bands
And lying in a manger

13 All of a sudden
A great heavenly host
Was there with the angel
   Giving praise to God and saying
14   Glory to God in the heights
      And peace on the earth
      Among men of good will

15 When the angels
Had gone away from them
Into heaven
   The shepherds said to one another
      Let us go to Bethlehem
      And see what has taken place there
      Which the Lord
      Has revealed to us

16   They came with all speed
And found Mary and Joseph
With the new-born babe
Who was lying in the manger

17   When they had seen it
They spread the news
Of what had been said to them
Concerning this child

18   And all who heard it
Were astonished
At what the shepherds told them

19   But Mary
Stored up all these things
Dwelling on them in her heart

20   And the shepherds returned
Giving glory and praise to God
As all
That they had heard and seen
Was just as they had been told

Jesus is circumcised

21   After eight days
He was circumcised
And he was given the name
Jesus
Which he was called by the angel
Before he was conceived in the womb

Jesus is presented in the Temple

22 When the days of their purification
Were completed
According to the law of Moses
They took him up to Jerusalem
To present him to the Lord

23 As it is written in his law
Every male who is the first born
Shall be called holy to the Lord
24 And to make an offering
As it is laid down
By the law of the Lord
A pair of turtle doves
Or two little pigeons

25 Now there was a man in Jerusalem
Whose name was Simeon
This man was upright and devout
Expecting comfort for Israel
And the Holy Spirit was upon him

26 He had been warned
By the Holy Spirit
That he should not see death
Before he had seen
The Lord's Christ

27 Lead by the Spirit
He came into the Temple
When the child Jesus' parents

Brought him in
To do for him
What was required of them
By the custom of the law

28   He took him into his arms
And praised God
    And said
29   Now Master
        Release your servant
        To go in peace
        According to what you have said
30   Because my eyes have seen
        Your salvation
31   Which you have made ready
        In the sight of all the peoples
32   A light of revelation
        To the Gentles
        And the glory of your people Israel

33   His father and mother
Were astonished
At what was said about him

34   Simeon blessed them
    And said to his mother Mary
        See
        This is the one who is destined
        To cause the fall and resurrection
        Of many in Israel
        And for a sign which is disputed

35 And a sword
Will also pierce your own soul
That the thoughts of many hearts
May be revealed

36 There was Anna
A prophetess
Who was a daughter of Phanuel
Of the tribe of Asher

She was advanced in age
Having lived with her husband
Seven years from her virginity
37 And then as a widow
Until she was eighty four years old

Now she did not leave the Temple
Serving night and day
With fasting and earnest prayer

38 Coming upon them
Just at that hour
She gave thanks to God
And she spoke about him
To all those in Jerusalem
Who were expecting their deliverance

39 When everything had been done
According to the divine law
They went back to Nazareth in Galilee
Which was their home town

40   The child grew
Becoming strong and filled with wisdom
And the grace of God
Was upon him

The twelve year old Jesus in the temple

41   His parents
Went up to Jerusalem every year
For the Passover Festival

42   And when he reached twelve years old
They went up to the festival
According to their custom

43   When the days
Were at an end
And they set out to return
The boy Jesus remained in Jerusalem
Although his parents
Did not become aware of it

44   But thinking he was in the company
They went a day's journey
Before they looked for him
Among their relations
And the people whom they knew

45   When they did not find him
They went back to Jerusalem
To search for him

46   And it so happened
That after three days
They found him in the Temple
Sitting surrounded by the teachers
Listening to them
And asking them questions

47   Everyone who heard him
Was astonished
At his understanding
And his answers

48   When they saw him
They were amazed
    And his mother said to him
       Child
       Why have you done this to us?
       See how your father
       And I myself
       Have been searching for you
       In great distress

49   And he said to them
       Why were you searching for me
       Did you not know
       That I must be in my Father's house?

50   But they did not understand
What he said to them

51 Going down with them
   He came to Nazareth
   And obeyed them
   But his mother
   Guarded all these things carefully
   In her heart

52 As he grew older
   Jesus progressed in wisdom
   And in the favour of God
   And of his fellow men

3 *The preaching of John the Baptist*

1 Now in the fifteenth year
  Of the government of Tiberius Caesar
  When Pontius Pilate
  Was governing Judea
  And Herod
  Was ruling as Tetrarch of Galilee
  And his brother Philip
  Ruling as Tetrarch
  Of the country of Ituraea and Trachonites
  And Lysanias as Tetrarch of Abilene
2 When Anna and Caiaphas
  Were the high priests

  Word came from God
  To John
  Son of Zechariah
  Who was in the desert

3 And he came into all the region
Of the Jordan
Preaching a baptism
To change heart and mind
For the forgiveness of sins

4 As it is written in the scroll
Of the words of Isaiah the prophet
A voice calling in the desert
Prepare the road of the Lord
Make his paths straight

5 *Every hollow will be filled up*
And every mountain and hill
Will be brought low
The crooked ways
Will be made straight
And the rough roads
Made into smooth

6 *And all flesh*
Will see the salvation of God

7 So he said to the crowds
Who came out
To be baptized by him
Offspring of vipers
Who warned you
To escape from the anger
Which is to come?

8   Therefore bear fruits
Worthy of your change of heart
And do not begin
To say among yourselves
We have Abraham as our father
As I say to you
God has the power
To raise up children to Abraham
Even from these stones

9   The axe is already laid
At the root of the trees
So that every tree
Which does not bear sound fruit
Is cut down
And thrown into the fire

10   And the people asked him
What should we do?

11   He answered them
Anyone who has two tunics
Should share with whoever has none
And anyone who has food
Should do the same

12   Tax collectors
Also came to be baptized
And they said to him
Teacher
What should we do?

13   He said to them
        Only carry out your instructions

14   Serving soldiers asked him
        We also
        What should we do?

    And he told them
        Do not intimidate anyone
        Or accuse them falsely
        And be satisfied with your pay

15 The people expected something
But they were all
Questioning in their hearts
About John
If perhaps he could be the Christ

16   But he answered them all
        I
        I indeed baptize you
        With water
        But there is one who is coming
        Who is stronger than I
        The thong of whose sandals
        I am not worthy to untie
        He will baptize you
        With Holy Spirit
        And with fire

17   The winnowing fan in his hand
And he will sweep clean
His threshing floor
And gather the wheat
Into the barn
But the chaff
He will burn with a fire
That cannot be put out

18   Giving advice to the people
In many different ways
He brought the good news

Herod puts John in prison

19   But Herod the tetrarch
When he was rebuked by him
Because of Herodias
His brother's wife
And because of all the wicked things
Which Herod had done

20   Added this above all
That he shut up John in prison.

The baptism of Jesus Christ

21   Now it happened
When all the people had been baptized
And Jesus had not been baptized
And was praying
That the heaven was opened

22   And the Holy Spirit
Descended on him

In visible form
As a dove

And a voice came out of heaven
>   You are my son
>   The beloved
>   Today I have brought you to birth

The ancestry of Jesus

23   And Jesus himself
Began his work
When he was about thirty years old
Being
As he was supposed
The son of Joseph
Who was the son of Heli

24   The son of Matthat
The son of Levi
The son of Melchi
The son of Jannai
The son of Joseph

25   Who was the son of Mattathias
The son of Amos
The son of Nahum
The son of Esli
The son of Naggai

26   Who was the son of Maath
The son of Mattathias

The son of Semein
The son of Josech
The son of Joda

27 Who was the son of Joanan
The son of Rhesa
The son Zerubbabel
The son of Shealtiel
The son of Neri

28 Who was the son of Melchi
The son of Addi
The son of Cosam
The son of Elmadam
The son of Er

29 Who was the son of Joshua
The son of Eliezer
The son of Jorim
The son of Matthat
The son of Levi

30 Who was the son of Simeon
The son of Judah
The son of Joseph
The son of Jonam
The son of Eliakim

31 Who was the son of Melea
The son of Menna
The son of Mattatha

The son of Nathan
The son of David

32 Who was the son of Jesse
The son of Obed
The on of Boaz
The son of Sala
The son of Nahshon

33 Who was the son of Amminadab
The son of Admin
The son of Arni
The son Hezron
The son of Perez
The son of Judah

34 Who was the son of Jacob
The son of Isaac
The son of Abraham
The son of Terah
The son of Nahor

35 Who was the son of Serug
The son of Reu
The son of Peleg
The son of Eber
The son of Shelah

36 Who was the son of Cainan
The son of Arphaxad
The son of Shem

The son of Noah
The son of Lamech

37 Who was the son of Methuselah
The son of Enoch
The son of Jared
The son of Mahalaleel
The son of Cainan
38 The son of Enos
The son of Seth
The son of Adam
Who was the son of God

4 *The Temptation*
1 Jesus returned from the Jordan
2 Full of the Holy Spirit

For forty days
He was led in the spirit
Through the desert
Tempted by the devil

And during those days
He did not eat anything
So that when they came to an end
He was hungry

3   And the devil said to him
               If you are God's son
               Tell this stone
               To become a loaf of bread

4   Jesus answered him
           It has been written
           Mankind
           Shall not only live on bread

5   He led him high up
    And showed him
    All the kingdoms of the civilized world
    In a moment of time

6   And the devil said to him
           I will give you
           All this authority
           And their glory
           Because it has been delivered to me
           And I may give it
           To whom ever I wish

7   If therefore
           You will bow down before me
           All will be yours

8   Jesus answered him
           It has been written
           You shall worship
           The Lord your God
           And you shall only serve him

9   He led him to Jerusalem
    And set him
    On the parapet of the Temple

And said to him
　　If you are God's son
　　Throw yourself down from here
10　　As it has been written
　　　He will command his angels
　　　To watch over you
11　　　*And on their hands*
　　　They will carry you
　　　Lest you strike your foot
　　　Against a stone

12　Jesus answered him
　　　It has been said
　　　You shall not
　　　Put the Lord your God
　　　To the test

13　When the devil
　　Had come to an the end
　　Of all the temptations
　　He went away from him
　　Until there should be an opportunity

Jesus preaches in Nazareth
14　Jesus returned to Galilee
　　In the power of the spirit
　　And there was talk of him
　　Throughout the countryside

15　He taught in the synagogues
　　And all the people praised him

16   He came to Nazareth
Where he had been brought up
And on the sabbath day
As was usual with him
He went into the synagogue
And stood up to read

17   A scroll of the prophet Isaiah
Was given to him
He unwound the scroll
And found the place
Where there was written

18   *The spirit of the Lord*
Is upon me
Because he has anointed me
To preach good news to the poor

He has sent me
To announce the release
Of those taken prisoner
To give sight to the blind
And liberty
To those who are oppressed
19   *To proclaim a year*
Which is acceptable to the Lord

20   When he had wound up the scroll
And returned it to the attendant
He sat down
And the eyes

Of all those in the synagogue
Were fastened on him

21 Then he began to speak to them
> And said
>> Today has this scripture
>> Been fulfilled in your ears

22 Everyone paid attention to him
And they were astonished
At the gracious words
Which came from his mouth

> And they said
>> Is he not Joseph's son?

23 He said to them
> You will certainly quote to me
> This proverb
> Physician
> Heal yourself
> We have heard
> What has happened in Capernaum
> Now do these things
> Here in your native place

24 And he said
> Certainly I say to you
> No prophet is accepted
> In his native place

25 But I am telling you the truth
There were many widows
In Israel
In the days of Elijah
When the heavens were closed
For three years and six months
And there was great famine
Over all the land

26 And Elijah
Was not sent
To any one of them
But to a woman
Living in Zarephath in Sidon

27 And there were many lepers
In Israel
When Elisha was a prophet
But not one of them
Was cleansed
Except Naaman the Syrian

28 All those in the synagogue
Were filled with anger
When they heard this

29 And they rose up
And cast him out of the town

They led him
To a ridge of the hill

On which their town was built
So that they could throw him down
Over the precipice

30 But he passed between them
And went away

A demoniac is healed in Capernaum
31 He went down to Capernaum
Which is a town in Galilee
And he taught them on the sabbath
32 They were amazed at his teaching
Because his words had authority

33 There was a man in the synagogue
Who had the spirit of an unclean demon
    And he shouted out aloud
34   Ah
        What is between us and you
        Jesus Nazarene?
        Have you come to destroy us?
        I know who you are
        The Holy One of God

35   Jesus spoke sternly to him
    And said
        Be silenced
        And come out of him

And throwing him down
Among them all

The demon came out of him
Without doing any harm

36 They were all astonished
    And said to one another
        What word is this?
        Because with authority and power
        He commands the unclean spirits
        And they come out

37 The echo
   Of what he was doing
   Went out into all the surrounding country

The healing of Simon's mother-in-law

38 He rose up
   And left the synagogue

   Then he went into Simon's house
   Where Simon's mother-in-law
   Was suffering from a high fever
   And they asked him about her

39 He stood over her
   And spoke sternly to the fever
   And it left her

   At once she rose up
   And served them

Jesus heals at sunset

40 When the sun was setting
All those
Who had anyone suffering
From any kind of disease
Brought them to him
And putting his hands
On each one of them
He healed them

41 And as the demons
Also came out of many people
They cried out and said
You are the Son of God

He silenced them
And would not allow them
To speak
Because they knew him
To be the Christ

Jesus preaches throughout the land

42 At day break
He went out to a desert place

The people searched for him
And when they came to him
They tried to prevent him from leaving them

43 But he said to them
I must also preach the good news
Of the Kingdom of God

In other towns
Because it was for this
That I have been sent out

44 And he preached
In the synagogues of Judea

5 *Simon's great catch of fishes*
1 It happened
When the people crowded round him
To hear the word of God
That he was standing
By the lake of Gennesaret
2 And he saw two small boats
Beside the lake
But the fishermen had left them
And were washing the nets

3 He embarked
In one of the boats
Which belonged to Simon
And asked him to put out
A little way from the land

Then sitting in the boat
He taught the crowds

4 When he had finished speaking
He said to Simon
Put out into deep water

And let down your nets
for a catch

5   Simon answered
        Master
        We have worked hard all night
        And have taken nothing
        But as you ask
        I will let down the nets

6   They did this
And enclosed a great many fishes
Tearing their nets

7   They beckoned to their partners
In the other boat
To come and help them
And they came
And filled both the boats
So that they were sinking

8   When Simon Peter saw this
He fell at the feet of Jesus
    And said
        Leave me
        Lord
        Because I am a sinful man

9   He was overcome with amazement
At the catch of fishes
Which they had taken

As were all those with him
10   Both James and John
The sons of Zebedee
Who shared with Simon

    Jesus said to Simon
        Do not be afraid
        From now on
        You will capture men

11   They brought the boat to land
And left everything
To follow him

The Healing of a Leper
12   He was in one of the towns
And there was a man
Full of leprosy

When he saw Jesus
He fell on his face
    And entreated him
        Lord
        If you will
        You are able to make me clean

13   Jesus stretched out his hand
And touched him
    Saying
        I will
        You shall be clean

At once
The leprosy left him

14 But Jesus impressed on him
That he should not tell anyone
    And said
        Go and show yourself
        To the priest
        And offer for your cleansing
        What Moses commanded
        As evidence to them

15 The news about him
Spread all the more
And large crowds went with him
To listen
And to be healed of their disabilities

16 But he withdrew into the desert
And prayed

The healing of a paralytic
17 It so happened on one of these days
When he was teaching
That Pharisees
And teachers of the law
Were sitting there
They had come from every village
In Galilee and Judea
And from Jerusalem

And the power of the Lord
Was in him to heal

18 Then there came some men
Carrying on a mattress
A man who was paralysed
And they made efforts
To bring him in
And to lay him down
In the presence of Jesus

19 Because of the crowd
They could not find a way
To bring him in
So they went up on to the roof
And let him down through the tiles
So that he lay on his mattress
Among them all
In front of Jesus

20 When he saw their faith
    He said
        Man
        Your sins have been forgiven you

21 The Scribes and the Pharisees
Began a discussion
    And said
        Who is this?
        He speaks blasphemies

Who has the power to forgive sins
Except God alone?

22 But Jesus
Knew what they discussed
   And answered them
      Why are you considering this
      In your hearts

23   Is it easier to say
      Your sins are forgiven
      Or to say
      Get up and walk?
24   Only that you may know
      That the Son of Man
      Has authority on the earth
      To forgive sins

   He said to the man
   Who was paralysed
      I say to you
      Get up
      And taking you mattress
      Go to your home

25 He rose up at once
In front of them
And taking the mattress
On which he had been lying
He went away to his house
Praising God

26 Astonishment
Took hold of them all
And they praised God

Filled with fear
They said
We saw strange things today

The calling of Levi
27 After this he went out
And beheld a tax-gatherer
Whose name was Levi
Sitting in the custom house
And he said to him
Follow me

28 He rose up
And leaving everything
Followed him

Jesus teaches in Levi's house
29 Then Levi
Made him a great feast
In his own house
Where a large number of tax-collectors
And of others
Were with them at the table

30 The Pharisees and the Scribes
Grumbled at his disciples
Saying

Why do you eat and drink
With tax-collectors
And with outcasts?

31 But Jesus answered them
It is not
Those who have good health
Who need a doctor
But those who are suffering
32 I have not come
To call the just
But the outcasts
To change their ways

33 They said to him
John's disciples often fast
And make requests in prayer
As do those of the Pharisees
But yours eat and drink

34 Jesus said to them
Can you
Make the bridegroom's attendants
fast
While the bridegroom is with them?
35 But the days will come
When the bridegroom
Is taken from them
In those days they will fast

36 He also told them a parable
No one
Tears a piece from a new cloak
To put it on an old cloak
Otherwise he will tear the new
And the patch from the new
Will not match the old

37 No one
Puts new wine
Into old wine skins
Otherwise the new wine
Will burst the old wineskins
It will pour out
And the wineskins will be destroyed
38 But new wine
Must be put into fresh wine skins

No one
Who has drunk the old
Wishes for the new
As he says
The old is better

6 *In the cornfields on the Sabbath*
1 It so happened
That on a sabbath
He went through the cornfields
And his disciples
Picked the ears of corn

And ate them
Rubbing them in their hands

2   Some of the Pharisees said
           Why are you doing this
           Which is unlawful
           On sabbath days?

3   Jesus answered them
           Have you not read
           What David did
           When he was hungry
           As were those who were with him

4   How he went
           Into the house of God
           And taking the loaves of offering
           Which it is not lawful
           For anyone to eat
           Except the priest
           He ate them
           And also gave them
           To his companions?

5   And he said to them
           The Son of Man
           Is Lord of the sabbath

The healing of a man with a useless hand
6   On another sabbath
He entered the synagogue

And taught
And there was a man
Whose right hand
Had wasted away

7 The Scribes and the Pharisees
Watched him narrowly
To see if he will heal
On the sabbath
So that they could find something
With which to accuse him

8 But he knew
What they were considering
    And he said to the man
    Who had the wasted hand
        Get up
        And stand in the centre

So he rose up
And stood there

9   And Jesus said to them
        I am asking you
        If it is lawful
        To do good or to do evil
        On the sabbath
        To save soul-bearing life
        Or to destroy it?

10   Then looking round at them all
          He said to him
              Stretch out your hand

      He did that
      And his hand was made good

11   They became utterly unreasonable
      And discussed with one another
      What they could do to Jesus

Jesus chooses the Twelve Apostles

12   It happened in those days
      That he went out
      On to the mountain
      To pray
      And spent the whole night
      In prayer to God

13   When the day came
      He called his disciples to him
      And chose twelve from among them
      Whom he named apostles

14   Simon
      Whom he also named Peter
      His brother Andrew
      James and John
      Philip
      Bartholomew
15   Matthew

Thomas
James son of Alphaeus
Simon called the Zealot
Judas son of James
16   And Judas Iscariot
Who became a traitor

The sermon on the plain
17   He came down with them
And stood on the level ground
With a large crowd of his disciples
And very many people
From all parts of Judea
And from Jerusalem
And the sea coast of Tyre and Sidon
18   Who came to hear him
And be cured of their diseases
Also those who were tormented
By unclean spirits
Were healed

19   Everyone in the crowd
Was trying to touch him
Because power came from him
Which healed them all

20   He lifted up his eyes
On his disciples
    And said
      Blessed are you
      Who are beggars

Because yours
Is the Kingdom of God

21 Blessed are you
Who are hungry now
Because you will be satisfied

Blessed are you
Who weep now
Because you will laugh

22 Blessed are you
When your fellow men hate you
And when they separate you from
them
And reproach you
And cast out your name as evil
For the sake of the Son of Man

23 In that day
Leap and rejoice
As indeed in heaven
You have a great reward
Because their forefathers
Did the same to the prophets

24 But woe to you
Who are rich
Because you have received
Your consolation

Woe to you
Who are satisfied now
Because you will be hungry

25 Woe to you
Who laugh now
Because you will mourn and weep

26 Woe to you
When all your fellow men
Speak well of you
Because their forefathers
Did the same to the false prophets

27 But I say
To you who listen
Love your enemies
Give help to those who hate you
28 Bless those who curse you
Pray for those who ill treat you

29 If anyone
Hits you on the cheek
Turn to him the other as well

And if anyone
Takes your cloak
Do not prevent him
From taking your tunic

30 Give to everyone
    Who asks you
    And if anyone
    takes your possessions
    Do not ask for them back

31 What ever you wish
    That your fellow men
    Should do to you
    Do the same for them

32 If you love those who love you
    What thanks should you have?
    Because even outcasts
    Love those who love them

33 If you do good
    To those who do good to you
    What thanks should you have?
    Because even the outcasts
    Do the same

34 If you lend
    To those from whom
    You hope to receive
    What thanks should you have?
    Because even the outcasts
    Lend to outcasts
    So that they may receive
    The same again

35 But love your enemies
And do good and lend
Never giving up
Then your reward will be great
And you
Will be sons of the Most High
Because he is kind
To the unthankful
And the wicked

36 You should be merciful
As your Father is merciful

37 Do not judge others
So that you
May not be judged
Do not condemn others
So that you
May not be condemned
Release others
And you will be released

38 Give
And it will be given to you
A sufficient measure
Pressed down
Shaken together
And running over
Will it be given into your lap
As it is the measure
With which you measure

That will be measured to you
In return

39   And he told them
This parable
    A blind man is not able to guide
    Another who is blind
    Or both
    Will fall into a ditch

40   A disciple
Is not above his teacher
But when he has learnt
Every one
Will be like his teacher

41   And why do you see
The splinter in your brother's eye
And do not pay attention to the beam
In your own eye

42   How can you say to your brother
Brother
Allow me to take the splinter
Out of your eye
When you yourself
Do not see the beam
In your own eye?

Hypocrite
First take the beam

Out of your own eye
Then you will see clearly
To take out the splinter
Which is in your brother's eye

43 Because there is no sound tree
Which produces rotten fruit
Nor is there a rotten tree
Which produces sound fruit

44 As every tree
Is recognized by its own fruit
They do not gather figs
From thorns
Nor from a thorn bush
Do they gather grapes

45 The good man
Brings forth the good
Out of the good treasure
Of his heart
And the evil man
Brings forth the evil
Because his mouth speaks
Out of his overflowing heart

46 Why do you call me
Lord
Lord
And not do what I say?

47   Everyone
Who comes to me
And who hears my words
And does them
I will show you
To whom he is like

48   He is like a man
Building a house
And when he dug
He went deep
And laid a foundation
On the rock
When there was a flood
The waters dashed against that house
And were not able to shake it
Because it was properly built

49   But whoever hears my words
And does not do them
Is like a man
Who built a house
On the earth
Without a foundation
When the waters dashed against it
It collapsed at once
And the ruin of that house
Was complete

7   *The healing of the centurion's slave*

1   When he had finished speaking
And the people had heard

All that he had to say
He entered Capernaum

2   Now there was a centurion
Who had a slave
Having fallen ill
He was about to die

The centurion valued him greatly
3   And hearing of Jesus
He sent elders of the Jews
To request him to come
And save his servant

4   When they came to Jesus
They begged him earnestly
    Saying
        You should grant this
        Because he deserves it
5   He loves our nation
        And built us a synagogue

6   So Jesus went with them

While he was still some distance
From the house
The centurion sent friends
    Who said to him
        Do not take the trouble
        As I am not worthy
        That you should enter under my roof

7
  Therefore I did not presume
  To come to you myself
  But speak the word
  Which says that my attendant
  Should be healed

8
  For I myself
  Am also a man under authority
  And I say to one
  Go
  And he goes

  And to another
  Come
  And he comes
  And to my slave
  Do this
  And he does it

9
 When he heard this
 Jesus was astonished at him
 And turning to the crowd
 Who were following
  He said
   I say to you
   In Israel
   I have not found such faith

10
 Returning to the house
 Those who had been sent out
 Found that the slave had recovered

The widow's son is restored to life

11 On the next day
He went to a town called Nain
With him
Were his disciples
And a large crowd

12 When he had almost reached the town gate
One who had died
Was being carried out
He was his mother's only son
And she was a widow
With her
There came many people from the town

13 When he saw her
The Lord had compassion on her
And said to her
Do not weep

14 He went to the bier
And touched it
The bearers stood still
And he said
Young man
I say to you
Rise

15 The dead man sat up
And began to speak
And he gave him to his mother

16 Fear took hold of them all
And they praised God
    Saying
        A great prophet
        Has risen among us
        And God
        Has visited his people

17 This was said about him
Throughout Judea
And in all the surrounding country

John sends his disciples to Jesus
18 John's disciples
Brought to him the news
Of all that had happened

Then John
Called two of his disciples
19 And sent them to the Lord
    To ask him
        Are you the one who is coming
        Or may we expect someone else?

20 When they came to him
    The men said
        John the Baptist
        Has sent us to you
        To ask
        Are you the one who is coming
        Or may we expect someone else?

21 In that hour
He healed many people
Who had diseases
Or suffered torments
Or had evil spirits
And he granted sight
To many who were blind

22 And he answered them
Go and give the news to John
Of what you have heard and seen
The blind have sight again
And the lame walk
Lepers are cleansed
The deaf hear
The dead are raised up
The poor receive the gospel
23 And all who do not reject me
Are blessed

Jesus talks to the people about John
24 When John's messengers
Had gone away
He began to talk to the people
About John
What did you
Go out into the desert
To behold?
A reed shaken by the wind?

25 But what did you
Go out to see?

A man wearing fine clothes?
Those who wear splendid clothes
And live in luxury
Are in king's courts

26 But what did you
Go out to see?
A prophet?

I say to you
Yes
And more than a prophet

27 This is he
Of whom it has been written
Behold I sent out my messenger
Before thy face
Who will make ready the road
In front of thee

28 I say unto you
Among those born of woman
No one is greater than John
But the least
In the Kingdom of God
Is greater than he is

29 All the people
And the tax-collectors
Who heard this
Recognized the justice of God
As they had been baptized by John

30 But the Pharisees and the lawyers
Rejected God's purpose for themselves
Not having been baptized by him

31 Then to whom shall I compare
The men of this generation
And what are they like?

32 They are like children
Sitting in the market
And calling to one another
We piped to you
And you did not dance
We mourned
And you did not weep

33 John the Baptist
Has come
Neither eating bread
Nor drinking wine
And you say
He has a demon

34 The Son of Man
Has come
Eating and drinking
And you say
Look
This is a man who is greedy
And a wine drinker
A friend of tax-collectors
And of outcasts

35   But wisdom
      Has been proved to be right
      By all her children

The woman who anointed Jesus

36   There was one of the Pharisees
      Who asked Jesus to eat with him
      So he went into the Pharisees house
      And took his place
      On a couch at the table

37   And now
      A woman living in the town
      An outcast
      When she learned
      That he was dining in the Pharisees house
      Brought an alabaster jar of ointment
38   And stood behind him
      Weeping

      She began to wet his feet
      With her tears
      And to wipe them
      With the hair of her head

      Then she kissed his feet
      And anointed them with the ointment

39   When he saw this
      The Pharisee who had invited him
      Said to himself

If he was a prophet
He would have been aware
What sort of woman it is
Who is touching him
As she is an outcast

40   But Jesus answered him
          Simon
          I have something to say to you

      And he said
          Teacher
          Say it

41   A certain creditor had two debtors
          One owed five hundred denarii
          And the other owed fifty

42   As they were not able to pay
          He pardoned both of them fully
          So which of them
          Will love him most?

43   Simon answered
          I suppose
          The one
          To whom the most was pardoned

      And Jesus said to him
          You have judged rightly

44   Then turning to the woman
        He said to Simon
            Do you see this woman?
            I came into your house
            And you did not give me
            Any water for my feet
            But she wet my feet
            With her tears
            And she wiped them with her hair

45   You did not give me a kiss
            But since I came in
            She has not ceased
            To kiss my feet

46   You did not anoint
            My head with oil
            But she has anointed
            My feet with ointment

47   This is my reason
            Why I say to you
            Her many sins have been forgiven
            Because she loved very much
            But the one
            To whom little is forgiven
            Will only love a little

48   And he said to her
        Your sins have been forgiven

49 Then those
Who were at the table with him
Began to say among themselves
 Who is this
 Who even forgives sins?

50 But he said to the woman
 Your faith has saved you
 Go in peace

8 *The parable of the sower*

1 And it happened soon afterwards
That he travelled
Through towns and villages
Preaching the good news
Of the Kingdom of God
And the twelve were with him

2 As were also some women
Who had been healed from evil spirits
And disabilities
Mary called Magdalene
From whom seven demons had gone out

3 And Joanna
The wife of Herod's steward Chuza
And Susanna
And many others
Who cared for them
Using their own resources

4   A great many people from the towns
     Had gathered together
     And when they came to him
         He said in a parable
5   A sower
             Went out to sow his seed

             And as he sowed
             Some fell beside the path
             And the birds of heaven
             Ate it up

6   And other seed
             Fell on the rock
             And when it grew up
             It withered
             Because it had no moisture

7   Other seed
             Fell among the thorn bushes
             And the thorns grew up with it
             And choked it

8   Other seed
             Fell on to the good earth
             And when it grew
             It produced fruit
             Increased a hundred times

     When he had said this
         He called out

Whoever has ears to hear
Should hear

9   His disciples asked him
What this parable could mean

10   And he said
         To you
         It has been given
         To become aware of the mysteries
         Of the Kingdom of God
         But for the rest
         They are in parables
         So that seeing
         They may not see
         And hearing
         They may not understand

11   Now this is the parable

      The seed is the word of God
12   Those beside the path
      Are the ones who hear
      Then the devil comes
      And takes the word
      From their hearts
      So that they may not believe
      And be saved

13   Those on the rock
      Are the ones

Who when they hear the word
Receive it with joy
But because they have no root
Although they believe for a while
In a period of trial
They fall away

14   Those who fell among the
         thorn bushes
Are the one who hear
And are choked
By the anxieties
And riches
And pleasures of life
So that nothing comes to perfection

15   Those on the cultivated ground
Are the ones
Who when they hear the word
Hold it fast
In a worthy and good heart
And bear fruit with endurance

16   No one
Who has lit a lamp
Covers it with a bowl
Or puts it underneath a bed
But on a lampstand
So that those who come in
See the light

17 As nothing is secret
Which will not be revealed
Nor concealed
Which will not certainly be known
And come out into the open

18 Therefore
See how you listen

Because whoever has
Will receive
And whoever has not
Even what he thinks that he has
Will be taken from him

The mother and the brothers of Jesus

19 His mother and his brothers
Came to him
But were not able to reach him
Because of the crowd

20 And he was told
Your mother and your brothers
Are standing outside
As they want to see you

21 But he answered them
My mother and my brothers
Are those
Who hear the word of God
And do it

Jesus calms the storm

22 One day it happened
That he embarked in a boat
With his disciples
    And he said to them
        Let us cross over
        To the other side of the lake
        So they set out

23 As they sailed he fell asleep
And a gale of wind
Came down on the lake
The boat was filling up
And they were in danger

24 They went to him
And woke him
    Saying
        Master
        Master
        We are perishing

But when he had been woken up
He spoke sternly to the wind
And to the rough water
It all ceased
And there was a calm

25   Then he said to them
        Where is your faith?

They were afraid and astonished
    And said to one another
        Who then is this
        Who can even command
        The winds and the water
        And they obey him?

The healing of the Gadarene demoniac

26 They sailed over
To the country of the Gadarenes
Which is opposite Galilee

27 As he disembarked on to the land
A man met him
Who belonged to the town
He had demons
And it was a long time
Since he had put on clothes
Nor would he remain in a house
But among the tombs

28 When he saw Jesus
He cried out
And fell down in front of him
    Shouting in a loud voice
        What is there between me and you
        Jesus
        Son of the Most High God?
        I pray to you not to torment me

29   As Jesus had commanded
The unclean spirit
To come out of the man

Because it had often
Taken hold of him
And although he was guarded
And bound with chains and fetters
He had broken the bonds
And been driven by the demons
Into the deserts

30   Jesus asked the question
         What is your name?

     And he said
       Legion

As many demons
Had entered him

31   And they begged him
Not to order them
To depart into the abyss

32   Now there was a large herd of pigs
Feeding on the hillside
And they begged him to allow them
To enter those pigs
And he allowed them to do so

33 So the demons
Came out of the man
And went into the pigs
Then the herd
Rushed headlong down a steep incline
Into the lake
And were drowned

34 When the herdsmen
Saw what had happened
They fled
And brought the news
To the town and the countryside

35 The people went out
To see what had happened
And when they came to Jesus
They found the man
From whom the demons had gone out
Now clothed
And come to his senses
Sitting at Jesus' feet
And they were afraid

36 Those who had seen it
Told them
How the one possessed by demons
Had been healed

37 And all the people
From the surrounding country of the
    Gadarenes
Asked Jesus to go away from them
Because intense fear
Had taken hold of them

So he embarked in a boat
And returned

38 The man
From whom the demons had gone out
Prayed to go with him
But he sent him away
    Saying
39   Go back to your home
       And tell them
       What God has done for you

And he went through the whole town
Proclaiming
What Jesus had done for him

Cure of a woman and Jairus' daughter is raised
40 Now when Jesus returned
The crowd welcomed him
Because they were all expecting him

41 And now there came a man
Whose name was Jairus

A leader of the synagogue
He fell at Jesus' feet
Praying him earnestly
To come to his house
42 Because his only daughter
Who was about twelve years old
Was dying

As Jesus was on his way
The crowds hemmed him in
43 And there was a woman
Who had suffered from severe bleeding
For twelve years
And whom no one
Was able to heal

44 She came behind him
And touched the fringe of his cloak
At once
The flow of her blood stopped

45 And Jesus said
Who is touching me?

When everyone denied it
Peter said
Master
The crowds are hemming you in
And jostling you

46   But Jesus said
     Somebody touched me
     As I
     I am aware
     That power
     Has gone forth from me

47 When the woman
Saw that she was not hidden
She came trembling
And falling down in front of him
She explained
In the presence of all the people
The reason why she had touched him
And how she was cured at once

48   And he said to her
     Daughter
     Your faith has saved you
     Go in peace

49 While he was still speaking
Someone came from the house
Of the leader of the synagogue
   And said
     Your daughter has died
     Do not trouble the teacher
     Any further

50 But Jesus heard this
   And answered him

Do not be afraid
Only believe
And she will be saved

51   When he entered the house
He would not allow anyone
To come in with him
Except Peter and John and James
And the father and mother
Of the child

52   Everyone was weeping
And mourning for her
    But he said
      Do not weep
      She has not died
      She is sleeping

53   They laughed at him
Because they knew
That she had died

54   But he took her hand
    And called
      Child
      Get up

55   Her spirit returned
And she rose up
And he instructed them
To give her something to eat

56 Her parents were astonished
But he ordered them
Not to tell anyone
What had happened

9 *The mission of the Twelve*

1 When he had called the twelve together
He gave them power and authority
Over all the demons
And to cure diseases

2 And sent them
To preach the kingdom of God
And to heal

3 And he said to them
Take nothing for the road
Neither a staff
Nor a bag
Nor bread
Nor silver
And do not each have two tunics.

4 Remain in what ever house you enter
Until you leave the place

5 And if anyone does not receive you
When you leave that town
Shake the dust off your feet
As a witness against them

6 So they went out
And travelled through the villages

Bringing the good news
And healing everywhere

Herod wishes to see Jesus
7 Herod the Tetrarch
Heard all that was happening
And was bewildered
Because it was said by some
That John
Had been raised from the dead
8 And by some
That Elijah had appeared
And by others
That one of the prophets from the past
Had risen again

9   But Herod said
        I myself beheaded John
        But who is this
        About whom I hear such things?

And he was anxious to see him

The feeding of the five thousand
10 When they returned
The apostles told Jesus
What they had done

Then he took them away
On their own
To a town which is called Bethsaida

11 But when the crowds
Became aware of this
They followed him

He welcomed them
And spoke to them
About the Kingdom of God
And cured those in need of healing

12 The day
Began to draw to an end
And the twelve came to him
  And said
      Send the people away
      So that they may go to the villages
      And to the farms round about
      Where they may find lodging
      And provisions
      Because we are here
      In a lonely place

13 He said to them
      You
      Give them something to eat

But they said
      We have only five loaves
      And two fish
      Unless we go away
      And buy food for all these people

14 There were about five thousand men

He said to his disciples
Make them sit down for a meal
In groups of about fifty each

15 They did so
Making them all sit down

16 He took the five loaves
And the two fishes
Then looking up to heaven
He blessed and broke them
And gave them to his disciples
To set before the people

17 They all ate
And were satisfied
Then they took up twelve wicker baskets
Of the pieces that were left over

Peter's confession of faith
18 Now it happened
That when he had been praying alone
His disciples were with him
And he asked them the question
Whom do the people
Believe me to be?

19 They answered
John the Baptist

But others say Elijah
And others
That one of the prophets from the
    past
Has risen again

20   And he said to them
        But you
        Whom do you
        Believe me to be

Peter answered
    The Christ of God

21   But he gave them strict orders
Not to tell this to anyone

First prophecy of the passion
22   And he said
        It is necessary
        For the Son of Man
        To have great suffering
        To be rejected by the elders
        The chief priests
        And the scribes
        To be killed
        And to be raised

23   Then he said to all
        If anyone

Has the will to come after me
He should not consider himself
But take his cross every day
And he should follow me

24   As whoever wishes to save
His soul-bearing life
Will lose it
But whoever loses
His soul-bearing life
For my sake
Will save it

25   Because what use is it to a man
If he gains the whole world
At the cost of losing or damaging
Himself

26   As whoever
Is ashamed of me
And of my words
The Son of Man
Will be ashamed of him
When he comes
In the revelation of his glory
And in the glory of the Father
And the holy angels

27   But I am telling you the truth
There are some standing here
Who will certainly not taste death

Until they see
The Kingdom of God

The Transfiguration

28 Then about eight days
After these words
He took Peter and John and James
And went up into the mountain
To pray

29 It happened that as he prayed
The appearance of his face changed
His clothing
Became as a lightning flash
30 And two men were seen
Conversing with him

They were Moses and Elijah
31 Who appeared in glory
And spoke of his exodus
Which he was about to achieve
In Jerusalem

32 But Peter
And those with him
Were heavy with sleep

As they woke
They saw the revelation of his glory
And also the two men
Who were standing with him

33   It was when they had parted from him
      That Peter said to Jesus
         It is right for us to be here
         Let us put up three tents here
         One for you
         One for Moses
         And one for Elijah

He did not know
What he was saying

34   But as he said this
There came a cloud
Which overshadowed them
And they were afraid
As they passed into the cloud

35   Then a voice
      Came out of the cloud
      Which said
         This is my Son
         Who has been chosen
         Hear him

36   After the voice had come
Jesus was found to be alone

They kept silent
And in those days
They did not report to anyone
Anything that they had seen

The healing of the demoniac boy

37 It so happened that on the next day
When they came down from the mountain
A large crowd met him

38 Then a man called out
From out of the crowd
Teacher
I beg you
To look at my son
Because he is my only child

39 As indeed
A spirit takes hold of him
And crying out
Suddenly throws him down
Foaming at the mouth
And after hurting him
It departs from him reluctantly

40 I begged your disciples
To cast it out
But they had not the power

41 Jesus answered
O perverted generation
Without faith
How long shall I be with you
And endure you?

Bring your son here

42   As he came close to Jesus
        The demon tore him
        And hurled him to the ground

        Jesus spoke sternly
        To the unclean spirit
        He healed the boy
        And gave him back to his father

43   And they were all astonished
        At the majesty of God

        Second prophecy of the Passion
44   As everyone was wondering
        At all that he did
            He said to his disciples
                Keep these words in your ears

                The Son of Man
                Is about to be betrayed
                Into the hands of men

45   But they did not understand
        What he said
        It was veiled from them
        Lest they should perceive it
        And they were afraid to ask him
        About this statement

Who is the greatest?

46 They entered into a discussion
Among themselves
As to which of them
Might be the greatest?

47 But as Jesus knew
What they were considering
In their hearts
He took a child
And stood him by his side

48 Then he said to them
Whoever receives this child
In my name
Receives me
And whoever receives me
Receives the one who sent me

Whoever is the least
Among you all
Is the one who is great

49 John spoke up
Saying
Master
We saw someone
Casting out demons
In your name
And we tried to prevent him
Because he does not follow us

50   But Jesus answered
        Do not prevent him
        As whoever is not against you
        Is for you

On the road to Jerusalem

51 Then
As the days of his ascension
Drew near
He set out
To go to Jerusalem
52 And sent his messengers ahead
To prepare for him

On their way
They entered a Samaritan village
53 Which did not welcome him
Because he was making for Jerusalem

54 When they saw this
    His disciples James and John
    Said
        Lord is it your will
        That we tell fire
        To come down from heaven
        And destroy them?

55 But he turned
And spoke sternly to them
56 And they went to another village

57 As they were on the road
  One of them said to him
    I will follow you
    Wherever you go

58 Jesus said to him
    The foxes have holes
    And the birds of heaven
    Have their dwellings
    But the Son of Man
    Has nowhere to lay his head

59 He said to another
    Follow me

  But he answered
    First allow me to go away
    And bury my father

60 Jesus said to him
    Leave the dead
    To bury their own dead
    But you
    You go and announce
    The Kingdom of God

61 There was another who said
    I will follow you
    Lord
    But first

Let me say goodbye
To those in my house

62   But Jesus said
            No one
            Who has put his hand to the plough
            And then looks back
            Is fit for the Kingdom Of God

10 *The mission of the seventy*
1   After this
The Lord appointed seventy others
An sent them out two by two
To go ahead of him
Into every town and place
Where he himself was coming

2   And he said to them
            Indeed there is a great harvest
            But there are few labourers
            Therefore pray the lord of the harvest
            To speed labourers into his harvest

3   Go forth
            See how I send you out
            Like lambs among wolves

4   Do not carry a purse
            Nor a bag
            Nor sandals

And greet no one
On the road

5 When you go into a house
First say
Peace be to this house
6 And if a son of peace
Is present there
Your peace shall rest on him
If otherwise
It shall return to you

7 Stay on in the same house
Eating and drinking with them
What ever they have
Because the workman deserves his
   wage
Do not remove from house to house

8 When you enter a town
And you are welcomed
Eat what is set before you
9 Heal the sick who are there
And say to them
The Kingdom of God
Has come close to you

10 But when you enter a town
And you are not welcomed
11 Go out into the streets
And say

Even the dust of your town
Which sticks to our feet
We wipe off on to you
However
You should be aware of this
That the Kingdom of God
Has come close

12   I say to you
That on that day
It will be more bearable for Sodom
Than for that town

13   Woe to you
Chorazin
Woe to you
Bethsaida
Because if the powerful deeds
Had been done in Tyre and Sidon
Which have been done in you
They would have altered long ago
Sitting in sackcloth and ashes

14   However
At the judgment
It will be more bearable
For Tyre and Sidon
Than for you

15   And you Capernaum
Were you lifted up

As far as heaven?
You shall go down
As far as Hades

16   Whoever listens to you
Listens to me
And whoever rejects you
Rejects me
And whoever rejects me
Rejects the one who sent me

Return of the seventy

17   The seventy
Returned with joy
    Saying
        Lord
        Even the demons
        Surrender to us in your name

18   And he said to them
        I perceived Satan
        Fall as lightning
        Out of heaven

19   See how I have given to you
The authority
To tread on snakes and scorpions
And on all the power
Of the enemy
And there is nothing
That will hurt you in any way

20   However
    Do not be glad
    That the spirits submit to you
    But be glad
    That your names
    Have been written in the heavens

Jesus prays to the Father

21 In that very hour
He was filled
With the joy of the Holy Sprit
  And said
    I give praise to you
    Father
    Lord of Heaven
    And of Earth
    Because you have hidden these things
    From the wise and the able
    And have revealed them to babes
    Yes Father
    As thus it was pleasing in your sight

22   All things
    Were handed over to me
    By my Father
    And no one understands
    Who the Son is
    Except the Father
    And who the Father is
    Except the Son
    And those to whom

It is the will of the Son
To reveal him

23 He turned to his disciples
Saying only to them
Blessed are the eyes
Which see the things which you see

24 As I say to you
That many prophets and kings
Wished to have sight
Of the things which you see
But did not have sight of them
And to hear
The things which you hear
But did not hear them

The good Samaritan
25 Now there was a lawyer
Who stood up to test him
Saying
Teacher
What shall I do
So that I may inherit life
Throughout the ages

26 Jesus said to him
What has been written in the law
How do you read it?

27 And he answered
You shall love the Lord your God
From all your heart
And with all your soul
And with all your strength
And with all your mind
And your neighbour as yourself

28 He said to him
You have given the right answer
Do this and you will live

29 But as he wanted
To do himself justice
He said to Jesus
And who is my neighbour?

30 Jesus took up what he had said
And replied
There was a man
Who was going down from Jerusalem
To Jericho
When he fell in with robbers
Who stripped him
And after raining blows on him
Went away
Leaving him half dead

31 Just then
There was a priest
Who came down that road

And when he saw him
Went past on the other side

32   There was also a Levite
Who came to the place
And when he saw him
Went past on the other side

33   But there was a Samaritan
Travelling on the road
Who came upon him
And when he saw him
Was filled with compassion

34   Going to him
He bound up his wounds
Pouring on oil and wine
Then he put him on his own mount
Brought him to an inn
And took care of him

35   On the next day
He took out two denarii
And gave them to the innkeeper
Saying
Take care of him
And if you spend more
When I myself return
I will repay you

36   Which of these three
        Do you think
        Became a neighbour to the man
        Who fell among the robbers?

37 He said
        The one who was merciful to him

    Jesus said to him
        Go
        And do the same yourself

Martha and Mary
38 As they went on their way
    He came to a village
    Where a woman
    Whose name was Martha
    Welcomed him into her home

39 She had a sister
    Called Mary
    Who sat by the Lord
    At his feet
    And listened to his words

40 But as Martha
    Was distracted by so much serving
        She came to him
        And said
            Lord
            Does it matter to you

That my sister
Has left me to serve alone?
Therefore say to her
That she should help me

41 The Lord answered her
Martha
Martha
You are anxious and worried
About all sorts of things
But few are necessary
Indeed only one
Mary
Has chosen the good part
Which shall not be taken away from
her

11 *The Lord's Prayer*
1 And it happened
As he was praying somewhere
When he had come to an end
One of his disciples said to him
Lord
Teach us to pray
Just as John
Taught his disciples

2 And he said to them
When you pray
Say

FATHER
MAY YOUR NAME BE KEPT HOLY
YOUR KINGDOM COME
3   THE BREAD WE NEED EVERY DAY
GIVE US EACH DAY
4   ANA FORGIVE US OUR DEBTS
AS WE OURSELVES FORGIVE EVERYONE
WHO IS INDEBTED TO US
AND DO NOT BRING US TO THE TEST

Teaching about prayer

5   Then he said to them
        Which of you
        Who has a friend
        Would go to him at midnight
        And say to him
        Friend
        Lend me three loaves

6   Because a friend of mine
        Has arrived on a visit to me
        And I have nothing
        With which to serve him

7   And the one inside would answer
        Do not trouble me
        Now that the door is shut
        And my children
        Are with me in bed
        I cannot get up
        To give them to you?

8   I say to you
     Even if he will not get up
     And give them to him
     Because he is his friend
     Because of his demands
     He will get up
     And give him as many as he needs

9   And I myself say to you
     Ask
     And it will be given to you
     Seek
     And you will find
     Knock
     And it will be opened for you

10   As everyone who asks
     Receives
     And the one who seeks
     Finds
     And for the one who knocks
     It will be opened

11   Which of you who is a father
     When his son asks for a fish
     Instead of a fish
     Would give him a snake?
12   Or if he asks for an egg
     Would give him a scorpion?

13   Therefore
If you who are evil
Know how to give good gifts
To your children
How much more
Will the heavenly Father
Give the Holy Spirit
To those who ask him

Casting out demons

14 He was casting out a demon
Which was dumb
And it happened
That as the demon left him
The dumb man spoke
And the crowds were astonished

15   But some of them said
    He casts out demons
    By Beelzebub
    The ruler of demons

16 And others
In order to test him
Asked him for a sign
Out of heaven

17 But he knew their thoughts
   And said to them
      Every Kingdom
      Which is divided against itself
      Is made a desert
      And a household against a household
      Falls
18   And if Satan
      Was divided against himself
      How would his Kingdom stand?

19   But if I
      I cast our demons
      By Beelzebub
      By whom to your sons
      Cast them out
      Therefore
      They shall be your judges

20   But if I
      I cast out demons
      By the finger of God
      Then the Kingdom of God
      Has come upon you

21   When a strong man
      Who is fully armed
      Guards his own forecourt
      His possessions are safe

22   But when one who is stronger
      Comes upon him
      And wins the victory over him
      He takes away his armour
      In which he put his trust
      And distributes the spoil

23   The one who is not with me
      Is against me
      And whoever
      Does not gather with me
      Scatters

24   When the unclean spirit
      Has gone out of a man
      He goes through waterless places
      Looking for rest
      When he does not find it
      He says
      I will go back to my house
      Which is where I came from

25   When he comes
      He finds it swept
      And put in order

26   Then he takes seven other spirits
      More evil than himself
      And goes in there to stay
      So the last state of that man
      Becomes worse than the first

27 It happened as he said this
That a woman in the crowd
Called out to him
Blessed is the womb
That bore you
And the breasts
That you have sucked

28 But he said
Indeed
It is rather those
Who hear the word of God
And who keep to it
Who are blessed

The sign of Jonah

29 As the crowds gathered round him
He started saying
This generation
Is an evil generation
It looks out for a sign
But no sign
Will be given to it
Except the sign of Jonah

30 Just as Jonah
Became a sign to the Ninevites
So will the Son of Man
Become to this generation

31
At the judgment
The Queen of the South
Will rise up
With the men of this generation
And will condemn them
As she came
From the bounds of the earth
To hear the wisdom of Solomon
And now
Here is one
Who is greater than Solomon

32
At the judgment
The men of Nineveh
Will rise up with this generation
And will condemn it
As they changed their ways
At the preaching of Jonah
And now
Here is one
Who is greater than Jonah

33
No one
Who has lit a lamp
Keeps it hidden
Or puts it under a corn measure
But on the lamp stand
So that those who come in
See the light

34
The lamp of your body
Is the eye
When the eye sees clearly
The whole of your body
Will also shine
But if it sees falsely
Your body will also be dark

35
Therefore keep watch
That the light which is in you
Is not darkness

36
If then all your body
Is shining
And has no part that is dark
It will shine
As if a lamp with its flashing
Enlightens you

Woe to the Pharisees and the lawyers
37
After Jesus had spoken
A Pharisee
Invited him to eat with him

So he went in
And sat down at the table

38   But the Pharisee was astonished
     When he saw
     That he had not first washed
     Before the meal

39   But the Lord said to him
             Now you Pharisees
             Clean the outside
             Of the cup and the dish
             But within
             You are full of grasping
             And wickedness

40   That is senseless
             Has not the one
             Who made the outside
             Also made the inside?

41   But give generously
             From what you have
             Then indeed
             Everything will be clean for you

42   But woe to you Pharisees
             Because you take a tenth
             Of peppermint and rue
             And every other herb
             And pass by judgment
             And the love of God
             These are the things you should do
             While not neglecting the others

43 Woe to you Pharisees
Because you love
The first seats in the synagogues
And greetings in the public places

44 Woe to you
Because you are like tombs
Which are not noticed
And men walking over them
Do not know that they are there

45 In response
One of the lawyers said to him
Teacher
When you say such things
You also insult us

46 And he said
Woe to you also
Lawyers
Because you burden men
With burdens
Which are hard to bear
But you
Do not touch the burden
With one of your fingers

47 Woe to you
Because you build the tombs
Of the prophets
And your fathers killed them

48 Therefore you are witnesses
And support the deeds of your
   fathers
Because they killed them
And you build their tombs

49 As it was said
By the wisdom of God
I will send to them
Prophets and apostles
And some they will kill and persecute
So that the blood of all the prophets
50 Poured out
From the foundation of the world
May be demanded of this generation

51 From the blood of Abel
To the blood of Zechariah
Destroyed between the altar of
   sacrifice
And the House of the Lord
Yes I tell you
It will be demanded of this
   generation

52 Woe to you lawyers
Because you
Have taken the key of knowledge
And not having entered yourselves
You have prevented others
From entering

53 When he left there
The scribes and Pharisees
Began to be terribly angry
And tried to make him speak
About very many things

54 Lying in wait
To catch him out
In what he said

12 *Jesus warns his disciples*

1 In the meantime
When thousands of people
Had gathered together
So that they even trod on one another
He first said to his disciples
Guard yourselves
Against the yeast of the Pharisees
Which is hypocrisy

2 Nothing is covered up
Which will not be uncovered
Or secret
Which will not become known

3 So what you have said
In the dark
Will be heard
In the light
And what was spoken by you
In the inner room

Will be proclaimed
On the rooftops

4   And I say to you
My friends
Do not be afraid
Of those who kill the body
And afterwards
Have nothing more
That they can do

5   But I will warn you
Whom you should fear
Fear the one who kills
And afterwards
Has the authority
To cast into the valley of burning
I say to you
That is the one you should fear

6   Are not five sparrows
Sold for two small copper coins
And not one of them
Has been forgotten
In the sight of God

7   And on your head
Even the hairs
Have all been counted

Do not be afraid
You are worth more
Than many sparrows

8   But I say to you
That anyone
Who acknowledges me
In the presence of men
The Son of Man
Will acknowledge him
In the presence
Of the angels of God

9   And whoever disowns me
In the presence of men
Will be disowned
In the presence
Of the angels of God

10   And everyone
Who says a word
Against the Son of Man
Will be forgiven
But whoever blasphemes
Against the Holy Spirit
Will not be forgiven

11   When they bring you
Before the synagogues
And before rulers and authorities
Do not be anxious

About how to answer
Or what you should say
12 As in that hour
The Holy Spirit
Will teach you what you should say

Parable of the rich landowner

13 Someone from among the crowd
Said to him
Teacher
Order my brother
To divide the inheritance with me

14 But he said to him
Man
Who has appointed me
As judge or divider among you?

15 Then he said to them
Watch out
And guard against all greed
Because no one's life
Consists in the amount that he owns

16 And he told them a parable
There was a certain rich man
Whose land was fruitful
And he said to himself
17 What shall I do
Because I have nowhere
To store my harvest?

18   So he said
        This is what I will do
        I will pull down my barns
        And build larger ones
        There I will store my wheat
        And all my goods

19   Then I will say to my living soul
        Soul
        You have many good things
        Stored up for the years to come
        Take your ease
        Eat and drink
        And be happy

20   But God said to him
        Senseless man
        In this night
        They will reclaim your living soul
        From you
        Then who will possess
        What you have prepared?

21   Such is the one
        Who has treasure for himself
        But is not rich in the realm of God

Trust in God
22   And he said to his disciples
            Therefore I will tell you
            Do not be anxious

About what you should eat
To support your life
Or about what you should wear
To clothe your body

23   The soul-bearing life
Is more than food
And the body more than clothes

24   Consider the ravens
How they do not sow or reap
And have neither a store house
Nor a barn
But God feeds them
How much more are you worth
Than the birds?

25   But which of you
By his concern
Can alter the way he is made?

26   If you have not the power
To do the smallest thing
Why are you anxious
About the rest?

27   Consider the lilies
How they neither spin nor weave
But I say to you
That Solomon in all his glory
Was not robed like one of them

28   And if in the fields
Where there is grass today
Which tomorrow
Will be thrown into an oven
It was clothed in this way
By God
How much more will he clothe you
You that have little faith

29   Do not look out
For what you should eat
Or what you should drink
And do not have them
On your mind

30   In all the nations of the world
People run after these things
But your Father
Knows that you need them

31   Instead
Look for his Kingdom
And all these things
Will be yours also

32   Do not be afraid
Little flock
Because it has pleased your Father
To give you the Kingdom

33 Sell what you have
And give to those
Who are in need
Make purses for yourselves
Which will not wear out
And have treasure in the heavens
Which will not fail
Where no thief comes near
And no moth destroys

34 Because where your treasure is
There your heart
Will be also

Be watchful

35 Tuck up your tunics
And have your lamps burning

36 Be like men
Who are expecting their Lord
So that when he returns
From the marriage
And comes knocking
They open to him at once

37 Blessed are those servants
Whom the Lord will find watching
When he comes
Certainly I tell you
That he will tuck up his tunic
And making them sit at table
He will come and serve them

38
If it is in the second
Or in the third part of the night
That he comes
And finds them watching
Blessed are those servants

39
Be aware of this
If the householder had known
At what hour the thief would come
He would not have allowed
His house
To have been broken into

40
So be prepared
Because it is at the hour
When you do not expect him
That the Son of Man
Will come

41
Peter said
Lord
Is this parable meant for us
Or for everyone?

42
And the Lord said
Who is that faithful and trustworthy
steward
Whom the lord
Will appoint over his household
To give them their measure of corn
When it is due

43   Blessed is that servant
Whom the lord
Will find doing so
When he comes

44   Certainly I say to you
That he will give him charge
Over all his possessions

45   But if that servant
Says in his heart
My lord delays his coming
And begins to hit the menservants
And the maidservants
Also eating and drinking
Until he is drunken

46   Then the lord of that servant
Will come
On a day which he did not expect
And in any hour
Of which he was not aware
And will cut him off
And his place
Will be among the unbelievers

47   But that servant
Who was aware
Of the will of his lord
But has not made preparation
Or acted according to that will

Shall be severely beaten
48   While the one who was unaware
Although what he has done
Deserved a beating
Shall be beaten less severely

Because from everyone
To whom much has been given
Much will be required
And from those
To whom much has been entrusted
Even more will be asked

49   I came to cast fire
On the earth
And how I wish
That it was already lighted

50   I have a baptism
With which to be baptized
And how I am oppressed
Until it is completed

51   Do you think
That I came to give peace
To the earth?
Not so
But rather to bring separation

52   Because from now on
There will be five in one house

Who will be divided
Three against two
And two against three

53   There will be divisions
Father against son
And son against father
Mother against daughter
And daughter against mother
Mother-in-law against her daughter-
   in-law
And daughter-in-law against her
mother-in-law

Right Judgment
54   Then speaking to the crowds
He said
When you see a cloud
Rising in the west
Immediately you say
That a rain storm is coming
And it will happen

55   And when the wind
Blows from the south
You say
That there will be heat
And it will happen

56   Hypocrites
You know how to interpret

148

The face of the earth
And of the heavens
But this present season
You cannot interpret

57   And why do you yourselves
Not make the right judgment?

58   As you go with your opponent
To a magistrate
Take the trouble
To be freed from him
While you are on the road
Or else he
May drag you to the judge
And the judge
Will throw you into prison

59   I say to you
That is certain
You will not come out of there
Until you have paid
The last copper

13   *The death of the Galileans*
1   At that same season
There were people present
Who gave him the news of Galileans
Whose blood
Pilate had mixed with their sacrifices

2 He answered them
   Do you think that those Galileans
   Were more sinful
   Than all other Galileans
   Because they suffered in this way?

3 No
   I say to you
   That unless you
   Change heart and mind
   All of you
   Will also perish

4 Or those eighteen
   Who were killed
   When the tower of Siloam
   Fell upon them
   Do you think that they were debtors
   More than all the men
   Living in Jerusalem?

5 No
   I say to you
   That unless you
   Change heart and mind
   You will perish
   In the same way

Parable of the fig tree

6 And he told this parable
   There was a man

150

Who had planted a fig tree
In his vineyard
And when he came
To look for the fruit
He did not find any

7 And he said to the vine dresser
For three years
I have come
To look for fruit
On this fig tree
And have not found any
Cut it down
Why should it use up the ground?

8 But he answered him
Sir
Leave it this year as well
Until I have dug round it
And spread manure
9 If it bears fruit in the future
Well and good
If not
Cut it down

Healing of a woman who was disabled
10 He was teaching
In one of the synagogues
On the sabbath
11 And now
There was a woman

Who had suffered from a disabling spirit
For eighteen years
She was bent double
And had not the power
To stand up straight

12 When Jesus saw her
He called her to him
    And said to her
        Woman
        You have been set free
        From your disability

13 He put his hands on her
And at once
She straightened up
And gave praise to God

14 Because he was indignant
That Jesus healed on the sabbath
    The ruler of the synagogue
    Said to the crowd
        There are six days
        On which work should be done
        So it is on them
        That you should come to be healed
        And not on the sabbath day

15 But the Lord answered him
    Hypocrites
    Does not each one of you

On the sabbath
Untie his ox or ass
From the manger
And lead them away to drink?

16   And should not this woman
A daughter of Abraham
Whom Satan has bound
For as long as eighteen years
Be set free from her bondage
On the sabbath day?

17   When he said this
All those who opposed him
Were shamed
And the whole crowd rejoiced
At all the glorious things
Which were happening through him

18   Therefore he said
To what can the Kingdom of God
Be compared?
And to what shall I compare it?

19   It is like a mustard seed
Which a man took
And threw into his garden
It grew into a tree
So that the birds of heaven
Nested in its branches

20   Again he said
        To what shall I compare
        The Kingdom of God?

21   It is like yeast
        Which a woman took
        And hid in three measures
        Of fine flour
        Until it was all leavened

Teaching on the road to Jerusalem

22   As he travelled through towns and villages
Teaching
And making his way to Jerusalem
23   Someone said to him
        Lord
        Will only a few be saved?

24   And he said to them
        Make every effort
        To go in through the narrow door
        Because I tell you
        That many will try to enter
        And will not succeed

25   When the master of the house
        Has got up and shut the door
        Then you will stand outside
        And begin to knock on the door
        Saying
        Lord open to us

And he will answer
I do not know
Where you have come from

26   Then you will say at once
We ate and drank in your presence
And you taught in our streets

27   But he will speak out
And say to you
I do not know
Where you have come from
Withdraw from me
All those who do what is unjust

28   There will be weeping
And gnashing of teeth
When you see Abraham
And Isaac and Jacob
With all the prophets
In the Kingdom of God
While you are thrown out
To the outside

29   The people will come
From east and west
To sit at table
In the Kingdom of God

30   But look
There are those who are last

Who will be first
And there are those who are first
Who will be last

31   In that same hour
There came some Pharisees
   Who said to him
      Leave here
      And go away
      Because Herod wishes to kill you

32   But he said to them
      Go and tell this fox
      See how I cast out demons
      And bring about cures
      Today and tomorrow
      And on the third day
      I shall be made perfect

33   However
      It is necessary for me
      To continue my journey
      Today and tomorrow
      And on the following day
      Because it is not possible
      That a prophet should perish
      Outside Jerusalem

34   Jerusalem
      Jerusalem
      Who killed the prophets

And stoned those sent out to her
How often
I wished to gather your children
As a bird gathers her nestlings
Under her wings
But you would not

35   Look how your house
Is left to you

I say to you
That you shall certainly not see me
Until it will be
Until you say
Blest is the one who comes
In the name of the Lord

14 *Healing of a man suffering from water retention*
1 It so happened that on a sabbath
He went to the house
Of one of the leading Pharisees
To have a meal
And they watched him narrowly

2 Now there in front of him
Was a man
Whose body was swollen

3   Jesus said to the lawyers
      And the Pharisees
            Is it lawful to heal on the sabbath
            Or is it not?

4   But they kept quiet

      Then he took the man
      And having healed him
      Sent him away

5   And he said to them
            Which of you
            Having an ass or an ox
            Which has fallen into a well
            On the sabbath day
            Will not pull it up at once?

6   They were unable to retort to this

      Humility and care for the poor
7   He told a parable
      To those who had been invited
      Because he noticed
      That they chose the best seats
            And he said to them
8   When you are invited by anyone
                  To a wedding feast
                  Do not sit down at the table
                  In the best seat

As someone may have been invited
Who is more valued than you are

9   Then your host
Who has invited you both
Will come and say to you
Make room for this man
So that you will be ashamed
And make your way
To the last place

10   But when you are invited
Go and sit down
In the lowest place
So that when your host comes
He will say to you
Friend
Go up higher
Then you will be honoured
In front of all those
Who are at the table with you

11   Because everyone who exalts himself
Will be humbled
And he who humbles himself
Will be exalted

12   He also said to his host
When you make a dinner or supper
Do not call your friends
Or your brothers

Or your relations
Or your neighbours
As they may invite you in return
And you will be repaid

13   But when you make a feast
Invite the poor
The crippled
The lame and the blind
14   And because they have nothing
With which to repay you
You will be blessed
And will be repaid
At the resurrection of the just

Parable of the great feast
15   On hearing this
One of those sitting at the table
Said to him
        Blessed is the one
        Who eats bread
        In the Kingdom of God

16   But Jesus said to him
        There was once a man
        Who made a great feast
        And invited many guests

17   At the time of the feast
        He sent out his servant
        To say to those who had been invited

Come
Because it is now ready

18 Then one and all
Began to make excuses

The first one said to him
I have bought a farm
And need to go out to see it
So I ask you
To have me excused

19 And another said
I have brought five yoke of oxen
And I am going to try them
So I ask you
To have me excused

20 Another said
I have married a wife
And therefore I am not able to come

21 The servant returned
And brought this news
To his lord
Then the master of the house
Became angry
And said to his servant
Go out quickly
Into the streets of the city
And bring in here

The poor
The crippled
The blind and the lame

22   And the servant said
Sir
What you ordered
Has been done
And there is still room

23   Then the lord
Said to the servant
Go out on to the highroads
And into the byways
And demand that they come in
So that my house
May be filled

24   As I tell you
That none of those men
Who were invited
Shall taste my feast

Following Christ

25   A large crowd gathered
And when they came to him
    He turned to them and said
26   If anyone comes to me
Who does not disregard
His father and mother

His wife and children
And his brothers and sisters
As well as his own soul-bearing life
He cannot be my disciple

27   Whoever does not carry his cross
And come after me
Cannot be my disciple

28   Which of you
Who intends to build a watch tower
Does not first sit down
And count the cost
To find out if he has enough
To see it through?

29   Otherwise
When he has laid the foundation
And has not the means to finish
Everyone who sees it
Will begin to taunt him
30   Saying
This man started to build
But was not able to finish

31   Or what king
Who is going to make war
On another king
Will not sit down and consider
If with ten thousand
He has the power

To meet the one who comes upon
   him
With twenty thousand

32   If he cannot
Ho will send out an embassy
To sue for peace
While that King
Is still a long way off

33   Therefore every one of you
Who does not take leave
Of all his possessions
Cannot be my disciple

34   Salt is useful
But if the salt becomes useless
With what will it be seasoned?
35   It is neither fit for earth
Nor for the manure heap
So it will be thrown outside

Whoever has ears to hear
Should hear

15 *The lost sheep*

1 Now all the tax-collectors and outcasts
Came to listen to him
2 But both the Pharisees and the Scribes
Were complaining a great deal
    And saying

This is the man
Who welcomes outcasts
And eats with them

3   Then he told them this parable
4   What man among you
Who has a hundred sheep
If he loses one of them
Does not leave the ninety nine
In the desert
And go after the sheep
Which has got lost
Until he finds it?

5   And when he has found it
He puts it on his shoulders
And full of joy
6   He returns home

Then he collects his friends
And the neighbours
And says to them
Rejoice with me
Because I have found
The sheep which I had lost

7   I say to you
That in heaven
There will be more joy
Over one sinner
Who changes both heart and mind

Than over ninety nine upright people
Who do not need to change

The lost coin

8 Or what woman
Who has ten coins
If she loses one coin
Does not light a lamp
And sweeping the house
Search carefully
Until she finds it?

9 And when she has found it
She collects her friends
And the neighbours
And says to them
Rejoice with me
Because I have found
The coin which I had lost

10 Even so I say to you
That in the presence
Of the angels of God
There is joy
Over one sinner
Who changes both heart and mind

The lost son

11 And he said
There was a man
Who had two sons

12   And the younger of them
    Said to his father
    Father
    Give me the share of the property
    Which should come to me
    And he divided the living
    Between them

13   After a few days
    The younger son
    Collected everything together
    And went away
    To a distant country
    Where he lived wildly
    And wasted his property

14   But when he had spent everything
    There was a severe famine
    Throughout the land
    And he began to be in need
15   So he joined one of the inhabitants
    Of that country
    Who sent him into his fields
    To feed the pigs

16   And he longed to fill his stomach
    With the pods
    Which the pigs were eating
    But no one gave him anything

17
When he came to himself
He said
How many of my fathers paid
workers
Have plenty of food
But here I
I am perishing with hunger

18
I will set out
And go to my father
And will say to him
Father
I have sinned against heaven
And in your sight
19
I am no longer worthy
To be called your son
Make me
Like one of your paid workers

20
He set out
And went to his father

When he was still a long way off
His father saw him
And was filled with compassion
So he ran
And falling on his neck
He kissed him warmly

21
Then his son said to him
Father

I have sinned against heaven
And in your sight
I am no longer worthy
To be called your son
Make me
Like one of your paid workers

22 But his father said to the servants
Bring out the finest robe
And clothe him
Put a ring on his hand
And sandals on his feet
23 Bring the calf
Which is being fattened
And kill it
Let us eat and be glad
24 Because this son of mine
Was dead
And has returned to life
He was lost
And has been found

They began feasting

25 But his elder son
Was out in the fields
And as he came near the house
He heard music and dancing
26 So he called
To one of the farm hands
To ask what this meant

27 And he answered
Your brother has come
And your father
Has killed the calf
Which was being fattened
Because he has received him back
Safe and sound

28 He was angry
And did not want to go in

So his father came out
And tried to persuade him

29 Then he answered his father
Look how many years
I have served you
And I
Never disobeyed your orders
But you
Never gave me a kid
So that I could feast
With my friends

30 But when this son of yours came
Who has wasted your livelihood
With prostitutes
For him
You have killed the calf
Which was being fattened

31   And he said to him
      Child
      You are always with me
      And everything that I have
      Is yours

32   It was right
      That we should feast and rejoice
      Because this brother of yours
      Who was dead
      Has returned to life
      He was lost
      And has been found

16 *The untrustworthy agent*

1   He also said to his disciples
        There was a rich man
        Who had an agent
        Of whom he heard complaints
        That he was wasteful
        With his property

2   So he called him
        And said to him
        What is this
        That I hear about you?
        Render an account of your
            management
        As you cannot be agent any longer

3   The agent said to himself
     What shall I do
     Now that the lord
     Takes the management away from
         me?
     I have not the strength to dig
     And I am ashamed to beg

4   I know what to do
     So that when I have been dismissed
     As agent
     They will accept me into their homes

5   And he called his lord's debtors
     One at a time
     And said to the first
     How much do you owe my lord?

6   And he answered
     A hundred measures of oil

     So he said to him
     Sit down at once
     Take your account
     And write fifty

7   Then he said to another
     And you
     How much do you owe?

And he answered
A hundred measures of wheat

So he said to him
Take your account
And write eighty

8   And the Lord
Praised the untrustworthy agent
Because he acted with forethought
And said
The sons of this age
Show more forethought
In their own generation
Than the sons of light

9   But I
I say to you
Make yourselves friends
By means of the unjust wealth
So that when it fails
They may receive you into tents
Which remain throughout the ages

10   The one who is faithful
In very little
Is also faithful in much

And the one who is dishonest
In very little
Is also dishonest in much

11   If therefore
        You were not faithful
        With unjust wealth
        Who will entrust to you
        The true riches?

12   And if you were not faithful
        With what belonged to another
        Who will give you
        What is your own?

13   No household servant
        Can serve two overlords
        As either he will hate the one
        And love the other
        Or he will hold to the one
        And despise the other
        You cannot serve God and riches

Christ answers the Pharisees

14 The Pharisees heard all this
    And as they loved money
    They scorned him

15   But he said to them
            You are the ones
            Who feel yourselves to be justified
            In the opinion of your fellow men
            But God
            Knows your heart
            Because what is highly thought of

Among men
Is an abomination
In the sight of God

16   Until John
There were the law and the prophets
Since then
The Kingdom of God
Is being preached
And everyone
Is pressing to enter it

17   But it is easier
For heaven and earth to pass away
Than for one detail
To fall away from the law

18   Everyone
Who releases his wife
And marries another
Commits adultery
And a woman
Who is released by her husband
And marries another
Commits adultery

The rich man and Lazarus

19   Now there was a man
Who was rich
And was accustomed to dress
In a purple robe

And in fine linen
And to eat splendidly every day

20 Lying beside his entrance
There was a beggar
Whose name was Lazarus

21 He was covered with sores
And he longed to be fed
With the pieces which were falling
From the rich man's table

Even the dogs
Came and licked his sores

22 It so happened
That the beggar died
And was carried away by the angels
Into the care of Abraham

The rich man also died
And was buried

23 In Hades
Where he was in torment
He lifted up his eyes
And saw Abraham
In the far distance
With Lazarus in his care

24   He called out
      Father Abraham
      Pity me
      And send Lazarus
      To dip the end of his finger
      In water
      To cool my tongue
      Because I am in deep distress
      In this flame

25   But Abraham said
      Child
      Remember
      That during you lifetime
      You received the good that was yours
      Just as Lazarus
      The evil
      But now he is comforted here
      And you are in deep distress

26   But as well as all this
      A great chasm has been fixed
      Between us and you
      So that whoever has the desire
      To pass over to you
      Has not the power
      Nor may anyone cross over
      From where you are
      To us

27 And he answered
Then I ask you
Father
To send him to my father's house
28 As I have five brothers

He should be a witness to them
And prevent them also
From coming to this place of torment

29 But Abraham said
They have Moses and the prophets
Let them hear them

30 And he replied
No
Father Abraham
But if someone from among the dead
Would go to them
They will change their hearts and
minds

31 But he said to him
If they do not hear
Moses and the prophets
Neither will they be convinced
If someone should rise again
From among the dead

17   *Christ teaches the disciples*

1   And he said to his disciples
          It is impossible
          That temptations should not come
          But woe to the one
          Through whom they come

2   It would be better for him
          If a millstone
          Were hung around his neck
          And he was cast into the sea
          Than that he should cause the
            downfall
          Of one of these little ones

3   You yourselves should take care

          If your brother sins
          Speak sternly to him
          And if he changes heart and mind
          Forgive him

4   And if he sins against you
          Seven times in the day
          And seven times he turns to you
          Saying
          I will change
          You should forgive him

5   The apostles said to the Lord
          Add to our faith

6   Then the Lord said
         If your faith
         Was the size
         Of a grain of mustard seed
         You would have said
         To this mulberry tree
         Be uprooted
         And planted in the sea
         And it would have obeyed you

7   Which of you
      Having a servant
      Who has been ploughing
      Or tending sheep
      Would say to him
      When he comes in from the fields
      Sit down at the table at once?

8   But will say to him
      Prepare my supper
      Then tuck up your tunic
      And serve me
      While I eat and drink
      After this
      You may eat and drink yourself

9   Does he thank his servant
      Because he carried out his orders?

10   In the same way
      When you carry out your orders

You too should say
We are not useful servants
We have only done
What was asked of us

Ten lepers are healed
11 As he was going to Jerusalem
He passed through the border
Between Samaria and Galilee

12 When he entered a village
Ten men met him
They stood some distance away
Because they were lepers

13 Raising their voices
They called out
Jesus
Master
Pity us

14 When he saw them
He said to them
Go
Show yourselves to the priest

Then it happened
That as they went
They were cleansed

15 But one of them
When he saw that he was cured
Turned back
Praising God with a loud voice

16 Falling on his face
At Jesus' feet
He thanked him
And he was a Samaritan

17 Jesus answered
Have not ten been cleansed
But where are the nine?
18 Was it only this outsider
Who turned back
To give praise to God?

19 And he said to him
Rise up and go
Your faith has saved you

20 When the Pharisees questioned him
Asking when the Kingdom of God
Was coming
He answered them
You cannot observe
The coming of the Kingdom of
God
21 And they will not say
It is here or there
As indeed

The Kingdom of God
Is within you

The coming of the Son of Man

22   And he said to his disciples
The days will come
When you will long to see
One of the days
Of the Son of Man
And will not see it

23   And they will say to you
Look there
Look here
But do not go after them
Or follow them

24   Just as the lightning flashes
Shining from one part of heaven
To the other
So the Son of Man
Will be in his day

25   But first
He must suffer greatly
And be rejected by this generation

26   As it was
In the days of Noah
So will it be also
In the days of the Son of Man

27 They were eating and drinking
Marrying
And giving in marriage
Until the day when Noah
Entered the ark
When the flood came
And destroyed them all

28 Just as it was
In the days of Lot
They were eating and drinking
Buying and selling
Planting and building
29 Until the day when Lot
Went away from Sodom
When it rained
Fire and sulphur from heaven
And destroyed them all

30 It will be the same
In the day
When the Son of Man is revealed

31 In that day
Whoever is on the housetop
With his belongings in the house
Should not come down to take them
And whoever is in the fields
Should not turn back

32 Remember Lot's wife

33   Whoever seeks to save
      His soul-bearing life
      Will lose it
      But whoever would lose it
      Will save it alive

34   I say to you
      In this night
      There will be two men
      In one bed
      One will be taken
      And the other will be left

35   Two women
      Will be grinding together
      One will be taken
      But the other will be left

36   Two men
      Will be in the fields
      One will be taken
      And the other will be left

37   They asked him
      Where
      Lord?

38   And he said to them
      Where the body is
      There the eagles
      Will gather together

18 *Parable of the determined widow*

1   He told them a parable
To show that they should always pray
And not give up

2   He said
In a certain town
There was a judge
Who neither feared God
Nor respected his fellow men

3   And in that town
There was also a widow
Who came to him
Saying
Defend my cause against my
opponent

4   For a time
He would not do it

But after a while
He said to himself
Although I do not fear God
Nor respect my fellow men
5   In the end
Because this widow troubles me
I will defend her cause
So that she no longer comes
To wear me out

6   The Lord said
                You should note
                What the unjust judge is thinking

7   Will not God
                Be patient with his elect
                And come to their defence
                When they cry out to him
                Day and night?

8   I tell you
                That at once
                He will come to their defence

                However
                When the Son of Man comes
                Will he find faith
                On the earth?

The parable of the Pharisee and the tax-collector
9   And he also told this parable
        To some who considered themselves
        To be in the right
        And looked down on the rest

10   Two men
                Went up to the Temple to pray
                One was a Pharisee
                The other a tax-collector

11 The Pharisee stood praying within
        himself
    And said
    God
    I thank you
    That I am not like other men
    Greedy
    Unjust
    An adulterer
    Or even like this tax-collector

12 I fast twice between sabbaths
    And give a tenth
    Of all that I receive

13 The tax-collector
    Standing far off
    Would not lift up his eyes
    To heaven
    But beat his breast
    And said
    God
    Be gracious to me
    A sinner

14 I say to you
    This man
    Went back to his home
    With his prayer heard
    Rather than the other
    Because everyone who exalts himself

Will be humbled
And whoever humbles himself
Will be exalted

Children are brought to Jesus
15 They brought babies to him
So that he could touch them
When the disciples saw it
They turned them away

16 But Jesus called them to him
    And said
        Allow the children to come to me
        And do not hinder them
        Because of such as they are
        So is the Kingdom of God

17   Certainly I say to you
        Whoever
        Does not receive the Kingdom of
          God
        Like a child
        In no way
        Will enter into it

The problem of riches
18   A leader among the Jews
        Put a question to him
        Saying
            Good teacher

What should I do
To inherit life
Throughout the ages?

19 Jesus said to him
Why do you call me good?
No one is good
Except God only

20 You know the commandments
Do not commit adultery
Do not kill
Do not steal
Do not witness falsely
Honour your father and your mother

21 But he answered
I have kept all this
From my youth

22 On hearing this
Jesus said to him
But there is still something wanting
Sell everything that you have
And distribute it to the poor
Then you will have treasure
In the heavens
And come
Follow me

23   When he heard this
     He grew deeply distressed
     Because he was enormously rich

24   Jesus looked at him
         And said
             How difficult it is
             For those who have possessions
             To enter the Kingdom of God

25   It is easier for a camel
             To enter through the eye of a needle
             Than for a rich man
             To enter the Kingdom of God

26   Those hearing him said
         Then who can be saved?

27   And he said
         What is impossible with men
         Is possible with God

28   Peter said
         See how we have left
         What belongs to us
         And have followed you

29   And he said to them
         Certainly I say to you
         There is no one
         Who has left house or wife

Or brothers or parents or children
For the sake of the Kingdom of God
30 Who will not receive much more
In this present season
And in the age to come
Life throughout the ages

Third prophecy of the Passion
31 He took the twelve
 And said to them
  Now
  We are going up to Jerusalem
  And everything will be completed
  Which has been written through the
  prophets
  About the Son of Man

32   He will be delivered to the Gentiles
  And will be mocked
  Insulted
  And spat upon

33   When they have scourged him
  They will kill him
  And on the third day
  He will rise

34 But they did not understand
Any of this
As what was said
Had been hidden from them

And they did not comprehend
These words

Healing of a blind man
35 Then it happened
That as he came near Jericho
There was a blind man
Sitting by the wayside
Begging

36 As he heard a crowd passing
He enquired what this meant

37 And they gave him the news
That Jesus of Nazareth
Was going past

38   He cried out
        Jesus
        Son of David
        Pity me

39 Those who went in front
Told him sternly
That he should be quiet

    But he cried out all the more
        Son of David
        Pity me

40   Jesus stood still
And ordered him
To be brought to him

As he came close
   He put the question to him
41   What do you want me
      To do for you?

He said
   Lord
   That I may see again

42   And Jesus said to him
   See again
   Your faith has saved you

43   Immediately
He could see again
And followed him
Praising the revelation of God

And all the people who saw this
Gave praise to God

19 *Jesus and Zacchaeus*
1   On coming to Jericho
He passed through it

2   And there was a man
Whose name was Zacchaeus

He was a high-ranking tax collector
And he was rich

3   He was anxious to see Jesus
To know how he looked
But he could not see him
Because of the crowd
And because he was small himself

4   When he had run on ahead
He climbed up into a sycamore tree
So that he could see Jesus
As he would be passing that way

5   On coming to the place
Jesus looked up
        And said to him
                Zacchaeus
                Come down quickly
                Because today
                I must stay at your house

6   He came down quickly
And welcomed him with joy

7   When they saw this
They all complained
        And said
                He has gone to stay
                With a man who is an outcast

8 Zacchaeus stood
    And said to the Lord
        Half of my property
        O Lord
        I give to the poor
        And if I have cheated anyone
        I return it four times over

9 And Jesus said to him
    Today
    Salvation has come to this house
    Because he too
    Is a son of Abraham

10 For the Son of Man
    Came to look for what has been lost
    And to save it

Parable of the ten servants
11 When they had heard all this
He also told them a parable
Because he was near Jerusalem
And they thought
That the Kingdom of God
Would appear immediately

12 Therefore he said to them
    There was a man of noble birth
    Who was going into a distant land
    To receive a Kingdom for himself
    And then to return

13   When he had called ten of his
         servants
He gave them money
Distributing among them
Ten silver minas
And he said to them
Trade with these until I come back

14   But his fellow citizens hated him
And sent a deputation after him
Saying
We do not want this man
To reign over us

15   It happened
That when he returned
After having received the Kingdom
He ordered those servants
To whom he had given the money
To be called before him
So that he might find out
From each one
What they had gained by trading

16   When the first came
He said
Lord
Your mina has gained ten minas

17   And he said to him
Well done
Good servant
Because you have been faithful
In very little
You shall have authority
Over ten towns

18   The second came
And said
Your mina
O Lord
Has made five minas

19   He also said to that one
You shall be over five towns

20   Then the other came and said
Lord
See here is your mina
Which I had stored away
In a linen cloth

21   I was afraid of you
Because you are a strict man
You take up
What you did not put down
And you reap
What you did not sow

22   He said to him
I judge you
By what you have said yourself
You bad servant

Did you know indeed
That I
I am a strict man
Taking up
What I had not put down
And reaping
What I had not sown

23   So why did not you
Give my money to the bankers
So that when I came myself
I could have claimed it back
With interest?

24   To those who were standing there
He said
Take the mina away from him
And give it to the one
Who has ten minas

25   And they said to him
Lord
He has ten minas

26   He answered them
I tell you

That everyone who has
Will be given more
But if anyone has not
Even what he has
Will be taken away

27   But bring those enemies of mine
Who did not want me
To reign over them
And execute them in my presence

The entry into Jerusalem

28   After he had said this
He led the way
Going up towards Jerusalem

29   And it happened
When he came to Bethphage and Bethany
Near the hill called after the olive trees
That he sent two of his disciples
    Saying to them
30   Go to the village opposite
And when you come into it
You will find a colt tied up
On which no man has yet sat
Untie it and bring it here

31   And if anyone says to you
Why are you untying it?
This is what you should say
Because the Lord needs it

32   Those who had been sent out
      Came and found everything
      Just as he had told them

33   While they were untying the colt
         The people to whom it belonged
         Said to them
            Why are you untying the colt?

34   They answered
         Because the Lord needs it

35   They brought it to Jesus

   And when they had cast their cloaks
   Over the colt
   They placed Jesus on it

36   And the people
   Spread their cloaks on the road
   As he passed

37   When he had almost reached
   The descent of the Mount of Olives
   The whole crowd of his disciples
   Began to rejoice with great shouts
   And to praise God
   For all the powerful deeds
   Which they had seen
      Saying
38   *Blest be the one who comes*

As the King
In the name of the Lord
Peace in heaven
And revelation in the highest places

39 Some of the Pharisees
Who were in the crowd
Said to him
  Teacher
  Speak sternly to your disciples

40 And he answered
  I tell you
  If these kept silent
  The stones would cry out

Jesus weeps over Jerusalem
41 As he came nearer
And saw the city
He wept over it
42 And said
  If only
  Even you
  Could know today
  What it is that brings peace
  But now
  It has been hidden
  From your eyes

43 As the day will come to you
  When you enemies

Will encircle you with a palisade
And oppress you on all sides
44 They will level you with the ground
Both you and your children
Who are within your walls

There is not one stone
Which will be left standing upon
    another
Because you did not recognize
The right moment
When it came upon you

Jesus clears the temple
45 When he entered the Temple
He began to turn out the traders
    Saying to them
46   It has been written
        My house
        Shall be a house of prayer
        But you yourselves have made it
        A robber's cave

47 He was teaching every day
In the temple
And the leaders of the people
Were looking for a way to destroy him
48 But they did not find anything
That they could do
Because the people
All hung upon his words

20 *Jesus questions the elders about John*

1   It happened one day
    That as he was in the Temple
    Teaching the people
    And preaching the Gospel
    The chief priests and scribes
    Together with the elders
    Came up and spoke to him

2   Saying
            Tell us
            By what authority
            Are you doing these things
            Or who gave you
            This authority?

3   He answered them
            I myself
            Will also ask for a word from you
            Tell me
4   Was John's baptism
            From heaven or from men?

5   They discussed it among themselves
        And said
            If we say
            From heaven
            He will say
            Why did you not believe him?

6   And if we say
            From men

All the people will stone us
Because they are convinced
That John was a prophet

7   So they answered
We do not know
Where it came from

8   And Jesus said to them
Neither will I
I say to you
By what authority
I do these things

Parable of the wicked farmers
9   He began to tell the people
This parable
A man planted a vineyard
And let it out to farmers
Then he went out of the country
For a long time

10   In due season
He sent his servant
To the farmers
So that they should give him
The fruit of the vineyard
But the farmers beat him
And sent him away with nothing

11   He sent another servant as well
But him they also insulted
And after beating him
They sent him away with nothing

12   He also sent a third
But they injured him
And threw him out

13   Then the owner of the vineyard said
What shall I do?

I will send my beloved son
Perhaps they will respect him

14   When they saw him
The farmers discussed it together
And said
This is the heir
Let us kill him
So that the inheritance
May be ours

15   Then throwing him out
Outside of the vineyard
They killed him

What therefore
Will the owner of the vineyard
Do to them?

16   He will come and destroy the farmers
       And will give the vineyard to others

       When they heard this
       They said
           May that never happen

17 Jesus looked at them
        And said
            What therefore
            Is this that has been written
            The stone which the builders rejected
            Has become the headstone of the
                corner

18   Anyone who falls on that stone
           Will be broken to pieces
           But anyone on whom it falls
           Will be crushed to powder

A question about taxes

19 At that same hour
    The chief priest and the scribes
    Made efforts to lay hands on him
    But they were afraid of the people
    Because they were conscious that this parable
    Had been told about them

20 They watched him narrowly
    And sent men
    Who pretended to be honest

To take hold of his words
So that they might hand him over
To the jurisdiction and authority
Of the governor

21   And they asked him this question
            Teacher
            We know that when you teach
            You speak out plainly
            Without regard to anyone's position
            But truthfully teach the way of God
22   Is it lawful for us
            To give tax to Caesar
            Or is it not lawful?

23 As he considered their trickery
            He said to them
24   Show me a denarius
                Whose is this portrait
                And inscription?

        They said
            It is Caesar's

25 And he said to them
            So give back to Caesar
            What belongs to Caesar
            And to God
            What belongs to God

26   Their position was not strong enough
In the presence of the people
To take up what he said
And marvelling at his answer
They fell silent

The Sadducee's question

27   Then came some of the Sadducees
Those who deny
That there is a resurrection
    To ask him the question

28   Teacher
        Moses wrote for us

If any man
Has a brother who dies
Leaving a wife but no children
Then that man
Should take his brother's wife
And raise up children
For his brother

29   Now there were seven brothers
And the first
Having taken a wife
Died childless

30   Then the second brother took her
31   And then the third

So that all the seven
Having died without children
Had done the same

32 Finally the woman
Also died

33 Therefore in the resurrection
Of which of them
Will she become the wife
Because all the seven
Had her as a wife?

34 But Jesus said to them
The sons of this age
Marry
And are given in marriage
35 But those considered worthy
To attain to the age to come
And to the resurrection of the dead
Neither marry
Nor are given in marriage

36 They are not able to die any more
But are equal to the angels
And are the sons of God
As they are sons of the resurrection

37 That the dead are raised
Was shown by Moses
At the thorn-bush

As he calls the Lord
The God of Abraham
And the God of Isaac
And the God of Jacob

38 He is not the God of the dead
But of the living

As indeed
All live to him

39 Some of the scribes
Answered him
Teacher
What you say is right

40 Because they did not have the courage
To ask him any more questions

Jesus questions the scribes
41 But he said to them
How is it that they say
The Christ is David's son?

42 Because David himself says
In the scroll of the Psalms
The Lord said to my Lord
Sit at my right hand
43 *Until I make your enemies*
A footstool for your feet

44   Therefore if David calls him Lord
             How is he his son?

45   All the people heard
      How he said to his disciples
46   Be on your guard against the scribes
            Who wish to walk about in long
                robes
            And who like greetings in the
                markets
            The first seats in the synagogues
            And the best places at meals
47   And who eat up the inheritance of
            widows
            And make pretence of long prayers

            They will be judged
            With greater severity

21 *The widow's offering*
1   He looked up
      And saw that the rich
      Were throwing their gifts into the treasury

2   Then he saw one poor widow
      Throwing in two of the smallest coins

3   And he said
            Certainly I say to you
            This poor widow
            Has put in more

Than all of them
4   Because their gifts
Came from what they have over
But out of her need
She has put in all the living
Which she has

Jesus prophesies disasters and persecution

5   When some people
Were talking about the Temple
Saying that it was made beautiful
By fine stones and votive offerings
    He said
6   You observe all this
The days will come
When there will not be a stone
Left standing upon a stone
Which will not be thrown down

7   And they questioned him
Saying
    Teacher
When will this be?
And what will be the sign
That this is going to happen?

8   And he said
    Watch out
That you are not misled
As there are many
Who will come in my name

Saying
I
I am

And also
The right moment is near

But you should not go after them

9 When you hear about wars
And revolutions
Do not be dismayed
As these things must first happen
But the end
Will not come at once

10 Then nation
Will rise against nation
And Kingdom
Against Kingdom

11 There will be mighty earthquakes
And in places
There will be plagues and famines
And there will be terrors
And mighty signs from heaven

12 But before all this
They will lay hands on you
And will persecute you
Giving you up to the synagogues

And to imprisonment
They will bring you before kings
And before governors
Because of my name

13 You will be landed with bearing
    witness
14 But hold in your hearts
That you need not practise your
defence

15 Because I myself will give you
Such grace of speech and wisdom
That all those who oppose you
Will neither be able to withstand
Nor to contradict it

16 You will be betrayed
By parents and brothers
And by relations and friends
Some of you
Will be condemned to death

17 Because of my name
Everyone will hate you
18 But not even a hair of your head
Will perish

19 It is through your patience
That you will gain possession
Of your living souls

20   But when you see Jerusalem
        Surrounded by encampments
        Then you will be aware
        That it will soon be desolate

21   Then those who are in Judea
        Should escape to the mountains
        And those within the city
        Should leave it
        While those should not go there
        Who are out in the country

22   Because these are days of vengeance
        When all that has been written
        Will be fulfilled

23   Alas for the woman
        In those days
        Who carries a child in her womb
        Or has one at her breast
        Because there will be great want
        Throughout the land
        And wrath upon the people

24   They will fall
        By the edge of the sword
        And will be taken as captives
        Among all the nations

        And Jerusalem
        Will be trodden down by strangers

Until the era of the heathen
Comes to an end

The coming of the Son of Man
25   There will be signs
In sun
And moon
And stars
And on the earth
Nations in distress
Anxious at the sound of the sea
And of the ocean surge

26   Men fainting from fear
And the expectation of what is
    coming
To the inhabited earth

27   Then will they behold
The Son of Man
Coming in a cloud
With power and great glory

28   When these things begin to happen
Stand erect
And lift up your heads
Because your deliverance
Is coming close

29   And he told them a parable
You observe the fig tree

And all the trees
30 When they put out leaves
You see for yourselves
And are aware
That the summer is now near

31 So also
When you observe these things
You are aware
That the Kingdom of God is near

32 Certainly I say to you
That this generation
Will not pass away
Until it will all happen

33 Heaven and earth
Will pass away
But my words
Will never pass away

34 But look to yourselves
Lest your hearts
Become burdened
With overindulgence
Drunkenness
And the cares of living

Because that day
Will come upon you suddenly
35 And trap you

218

As it will come on all those
Who are dwelling
On the face of the whole earth

36　　Be watchful at all seasons
Begging for strength
To escape all those things
Which are coming soon
And to stand in the presence
Of the Son of Man

37　Now during the daytime
He was teaching in the Temple
But at night he went out
And stayed on that hill
Which is called the Mount of Olives

38　Rising early in the morning
All the people came to him
To hear him

22　*The betrayal*
1　Now the festival of unleavened bread
Which is called Passover
Was coming close
2　And the chief priests and the scribes
Looked for a way to destroy Jesus
Because they were afraid of the people

3   Then Satan
     Entered into Judas called Iscariot
     Who was counted among the twelve

4   He went away
     And discussed with the chief priests
     And with the Temple officers
     How he could betray him to them

5   They were overjoyed
     And agreed to give him money
     Which he accepted

6   Then he looked for an opportunity
     To betray him
     Away from the crowds

Preparation for the Passover
7   When the day of unleavened bread came
     On which the Passover lamb
     Should be killed
8   He sent Peter and John
         Saying
             Prepare the Passover for us
             So that we may eat it

9   They said to him
             Where
             Do you wish us to prepare it?

10   And he told them
                Now when you enter the city
                A man will meet you
                Who is carrying a jar of water
                Follow him
                Into the house where he is going

                Then speak
11   To the master of the house
                Saying
                The teacher says to you
                Where is the guest room
                So that I may eat the Passover there
                With my disciples?

12   He will show you
                A large upper room
                Which has been set out ready
                Prepare for us there

13   They went
        And found everything
        As he had told them
        And they prepared the Passover

        The last supper
14   When the hour came
        He sat at the table
        And the apostles were with him

15   Then he said to them
        With great longing
        I have desired to eat this Passover
        With you
        Before I suffer

16   As I say to you
        It is certain
        That I shall not eat it again
        Until it is fulfilled
        In the Kingdom of God

17 He took a cup
And when he had given thanks
    He said
        Take this
        And divide it among yourselves
18   As I tell you
        From now on
        It is certain
        That I shall not drink
        The fruit of the vine
        Until the Kingdom of God comes

19 He took bread
And when he had given thanks
He broke it
And gave it to them
    Saying
        This is my body
        Which is being given for you

Do this
In memory of me

20   After the supper
He did the same with the cup
    And said
        This is the cup
        Of the new covenant
        In my blood
        Which is shed for you

21   But look how the hand
        Of the one who is betraying me
        Is with me on the table

22   It is certain
        That the Son of Man
        Will go
        According to what has been
            determined
        But woe to that man
        By whom he is betrayed

23   And they began to debate
Among themselves
Which of them it might be
Who was about to undertake
Such a thing

Rivalry among the disciples

24 And it happened
That there was rivalry among them
As to which of them
Should be thought
To be the greatest

25   So he said to them
          The Kings of the nations
          Are their overlords
          And those who have authority over
              them
          Are called benefactors

26   But not among you

          There the greatest
          Must become the youngest
          And the leader
          Like the one who serves

27   For who is the greatest
          The one sitting at the table
          Or the one who is serving?
          Surely the one sitting at the table
          But I
          I am among you
          As the one who serves

28   You are the ones
          Who have stayed with me
          Throughout my trials

29   And I
          I appoint you a Kingdom
          As the Father has appointed me
30   So that you may eat and drink
          At my table in my kingdom
          And you will sit on thrones
          Judging the twelve tribes of Israel

Jesus foretells Peter's denial
31   Simon
          Simon
          See how Satan
          Demanded to have you all
          To sieve out like wheat
32   But I
          I have prayed for you
          That your faith
          Might not fail
          And when you have come to yourself
          Support your brothers

33   And he answered him
          Lord
          I am ready to go with you
          Both to prison
          And to death

34 But Jesus said
    I tell you
    Peter
    Today a cock will not crow
    Until you have denied three times
    That you know me

35 And to all of them
    He said
        When I sent you out
        Without a purse
        Or a bag
        Or sandals
        Were you in need of anything?

    They said
        Nothing

36 Then he said to them
        But now
        Whoever has a purse
        Let him take it
        And whoever has a bag
        Should do the same
        And he who has no sword
        Should sell his cloak
        And buy one

37   Because I tell you
        In me
        The scripture is fulfilled

Which says
He was numbered with those
Who broke the law
As indeed
All that was written of me
Has an end

38 They said
Lord
See here are two swords

And he said to them
It is enough

Jesus prays on the Mount of Olives
39 On leaving there
He went to the Mount of Olives
As was his habit
And his disciples followed him

40 When he came to the place
He said to them
Pray
That you may not give way to
temptation

41 He withdrew from them
About a stone's throw
And he knelt down and prayed
42 Saying
Father

If it is your desire
Take this cup away from me
However
It is not my will
But yours
Which should be done

43 Then an angel from heaven
Appeared to him
Giving him strength

44 As he was in agony
He prayed ever more urgently
And his sweat
Became like clots of blood
Falling on to the ground

45 When he rose up
He came to the disciples
And found them asleep
Because of their sorrow

46 And he said to them
Why are you sleeping
Rise up
And pray
That you may not give way to
temptation

The arrest

47 While he was still speaking
They saw a crowd
Led by one of the twelve
Called Judas

He came up to Jesus
To kiss him

48 But Jesus said to him
Do you betray the Son of Man
With a kiss?

49 When those who were around him
Saw what was going to happen
They said
Lord
Shall we strike with a sword?

50 And one of them
Struck the high priest's servant
And cut off his right ear

51 Jesus answered
Let them have their way

And touching his ear
He healed him

52 Then Jesus
Said to the chief priests

To the captains of the Temple Guard
And to the elders
Who had come for him
    Have you come out with swords
    And with clubs
    As if against a bandit?

53   Every day
    When I was with you
    In the Temple
    You did not stretch out your hands
    Against me
    But this is your hour
    And the authority of the darkness

Peter's denial

54   When they had taken him
They led him away
And brought him into the high priest's house

Peter followed at a distance

55   In the centre of the courtyard
A fire had been lighted
And when the company sat down together
Peter sat down with them

56   One of the maidservants
Saw him sitting in the firelight
    And looking at him closely

She said
That one was with him

57 But he denied it
And said
Woman
I do not know him

58 After a little while
Another man saw him
And said
And you are one of them

But Peter said
Man
I am not

59 About an hour later
Another insisted
Saying
It is true
That this one also
Was with him
As he is certainly a Galilean

60 But Peter said to him
Man
I do not know
What you are saying

At once
While he was still speaking
A cock crew

61 The Lord turned
And looked at Peter

Then Peter remembered
What the Lord had said
When he told him
Before a cock crows today
You will disown me three times

62 He went outside
And wept bitterly

Jesus is mocked and beaten
63 Then the men who had taken Jesus
Mocked him and beat him

64 They blindfolded him
        And said to him
                Prophesy
                Which is the one
                Who is the one hitting you?

65 And blaspheming
They said many other things
Against him

Jesus before the Council

66 At daybreak
The assembly of the elders of the people
Consisting of both chief priests and
    scribes
Had Jesus brought before their Council
67   And said to him
            If you are the Christ
            Tell us

        And he said to them
            If I tell you
            It is certain that you will not believe
68   And if I question you
            You will certainly not answer

69   But from now on
            The Son of Man
            Will be sitting at the right hand
            Of the power of God

70   They all said
            Are you therefore
            The Son of God?

        And he answered them
            You say that I
            I AM

71   Then they said
            Why do we still need witnesses

As we heard it ourselves
From his own mouth?

23 *Jesus is brought before Pilate*
1   Then the whole assembly rose up
And brought him before Pilate

2   They began to accuse him
And said
        We found this person
        Misleading our nation
        Preventing us from giving tribute to
            Caesar
        And saying of himself
        That he is Christ
        A King

3   Pilate put the question to him
        Are you the King of the Jews?

    And he answered
        You say so

4   Then Pilate said to the chief priests
And to the crowds
        I do not find any crime
        In this man

5   But they persisted
And said
        He rouses up the people

Teaching throughout Judea
He started in Galilee
And then came here

Jesus is sent to Herod

6 When Pilate heard this
He asked
If the man was a Galilean

7 On discovering
That he came from Herod's district
He sent him over to Herod
Who was also in Jerusalem
During those days

8 When Herod saw Jesus
He was filled with joy

He had wanted to see him
For a long time
Because of what he had heard
About him
And he hoped to see some sign
Performed by him

9 He questioned him at length
But he did not answer

10 The chief priests and scribes
Stood by
Making great efforts to accuse him

11 Herod and his soldiers
Despised him
They threw a shining garment round him
And mocked him
Then sent him back to Pilate

12 On that same day
Herod and Pilate became friends
As before this
There had been ill will between them

Pilate fails to release Jesus
13 Then Pilate called together
The chief priests
The leaders
And the people
14   And said to them
        You have brought this man to me
        Because He is turning the people
        away
        But now I myself
        Have examined him in your presence
        And I do not find this man
        Guilty of the crimes
        Of which you accuse him
15   And neither did Herod
        As he sent him back to us

        So now
        As he has done nothing
        Which deserves death

16   When he has been disciplined
           I will let him go

17   But at the festival
      He had to release one prisoner for them

18   So the whole crowd cried out
          Take this man away
          And release for us
          Barabbas

19   Barabbas had been thrown into prison
      Because of some disturbance
      And murder
      Which had happened in the city

20   Pilate
      Called out to them again
      As he wished to release Jesus

21   But they shouted
          Crucify him
          Crucify him

22   He said to them a third time
          But what has he done wrong?
          I found nothing in him
          Which deserves death
          Therefore
          I will discipline him
          And let him go

23 But they held to it
And with loud voices
Asked for him to be crucified
And their voices prevailed

24 So pilate decided
That what they demanded
Should be carried out

25 He released the one
For whom they asked
A man who had been thrown into prison
For creating a disturbance
And for murder

But Jesus
He handed over to their will

The Crucifixion
26 As they led him away
They took hold of Simon
A Cyrenian coming from the country
And put the cross on him
To carry it behind Jesus–

27 A large crowd of people
Followed
Also many women
Who wailed and mourned for him

28   Jesus turned to them
        And said
                Daughters of Jerusalem
                Do not weep for me
                But weep for yourselves
                And for your children

29   Look
                The days are coming
                When they will say
                Blessed are the barren
                The wombs that did not bear
                And the breasts that did not give milk

30   Then they will begin
                To say to the mountains
                Fall on us
                And to the hills
                Cover us

31   Because if they do these things
                When the wood is green
                What will happen
                When it is dry?

32   Two others
        Who were evil doers
        Were led away
        To be put to death with him

33   When they came to the place
Which is called the Skull
There they crucified him
And the evil-doers with him
One on the right
And one on the left

34   Then Jesus said
            Father
            Forgive them
            Because they do not know
            What they are doing

So that they could divide his clothing
They threw dice

35   The people
Stood looking on
The rulers
Also scorned him
    They said
        He saved others
        Let him save himself
        If he is Christ
        The one chosen by God

36   And the soldiers
Mocked him
Coming up to him
And offering him vinegar
37   Saying

> If you are the King of the Jews
> Save yourself

38 There was also a superscription
Over him
THIS IS THE KING OF THE JEWS

39 And one of the evil-doers
Who was being hanged
>Blasphemed him saying
>>Are you not the Christ?
>>Save yourself and us

40 But the other
Spoke sternly to him
And said
>Do you not fear God
>Because you too have been
>sentenced?
41 >And we indeed justly
>Because the result of what we
>undertook
>Comes back to us
>But he has not undertaken
>Anything harmful

42 And he said
>Jesus
>Remember me
>When you come into your kingdom

43   He answered him
            Certainly I say to you
            Today
            You will be with me
            In Paradise

44 It was now about the sixth hour
    And there was darkness
    Over all the land
    Until the ninth hour
45 As the sun failed

    The veil of the shrine
    Was torn down the centre

46   And Jesus cried out
            With a loud voice
                Father
                Into your hands
                I commit my spirit

    As he said this
    He drew his last breath

47 When the centurion
    Saw what was happening
            He praised God
            And said
                This was certainly a just man

48 And the crowds
Who had come together at this spectacle
When they beheld what was happening
Beat their breasts and returned

49 All those whom he had known
Stood at a distance
Watching all this

With them were the women
Who had accompanied him
From Galilee

The burial
50 And now there was a man
Whose name was Joseph
He came from the Jewish town of Arimathea
And was a member of the Council

He was a good and just man
Who awaited the Kingdom of God
51 And he had not agreed
With their intention
Or with what they had carried out

52 This man went to Pilate
And asked for the body of Jesus

53 On taking it down
He wrapped it in linen
And placed it in a tomb

That was cut out of rock
And where no one
Had so far been laid

54 As it was a day of preparation
And the sabbath was approaching
55 The women
Who had followed him from Galilee
Took note of the tomb
And saw how his body was placed

Then they went back
To prepare spices and ointment

56 They remained quiet on the sabbath
As ordered by the commandment

24 *The Resurrection*
1 At day break
On the first day after the sabbath
They came to the tomb
Carrying the spices
Which they had prepared

2 And they found that the stone
Had been rolled away from the tomb

3 When they went inside
They did not find the body
Of the Lord Jesus

4   They were at a loss about this
When see
Two men stood by them
Clothed in lightening

5   As they were filled with fear
And bowed their faces to the earth
     The men said to them
       Why are you
       Looking for the one who lives
       Among those who are dead?

6   He is not here
       But has been raised
       Remember what he told you
       While he was still in Galilee
7   When he said
       The Son of Man
       Must be given up
       Into the hands of sinful men
       And be crucified
       To rise again on the third day

8   And they remembered his words

9   Then they returned from the tomb
To give the news to the eleven
And to all the others

10   Now it was Mary Magdalene
Joanna

Mary the mother of James
And the other women with them
Who told all this to the apostles
11 And their words
Appeared to them to be nonsense
So that they did not believe them

12 But Peter got up
And hurried to the tomb
He stooped down
And saw only the linen cloths
So he went home
Filled with wonder at what had happened

The road to Emmaus
13 On the same day
Two of them were on their way
To a village called Emmaus
Which was about seven miles from Jerusalem

14 And they talked to each other
About everything that had taken place

15 Then it happened
That as they were deep in conversation
And were discussing together
Jesus himself approached them
And travelled with them

16 But their eyes
Were prevented from recognizing him

17 And he said to them
What are the words
Which fly back and forth between
you
As you walk along?

They stood still
Looking depressed

18 The one who was called Cleopas
Said to him
Are you the only stranger in
Jerusalem
Who does not know
About the events which have
happened there
In recent days

19 He said to them
What events?

And they answered him
Those connected with Jesus
The Nazarene
A man who was a prophet
Powerful in deed and in word
In the sight of God
And of all the people

20 How both our chief priests
And our rulers

Handed him over
To be condemned to death
And crucified him

21 We were hoping
That he was the one
Who was about to ransom Israel

As well as all this
It is now the third day
Since it happened
22 And we were astonished
By some of our women
Who had been early at the tomb
23 And not finding his body
Came and reported
Having seen a vision of angels
Who said that he lives

24 Some of those who were with us
Went to the tomb
And found that it was indeed
As the women had said
But they did not see him

25 Jesus said to them
O you are senseless
And your hearts are so slow
That you did not believe
All that the prophets said

26   Was it not necessary for the Christ
      To suffer in this way
      And to enter into his glory?

27   And beginning with Moses
He went through all the prophets
Interpreting for them
All those parts of the scriptures
Which concerned himself

28   When they came near the village
To which they were travelling
He made as if to go further

29   But they persuaded him
      Saying
          Stay with us
          Because it will soon be evening
          And the day
          Draws to a close

And he went in
To stay with them

30   It happened
That when he sat at table with them
He took bread
And blessed it
And when he had broken it
He gave it to them

31 Their eyes were opened
And they recognized him

Then he was no longer
Visible to them

32 They said to one another
Did not our hearts
Burn within us
As he talked to us on the road
Explaining the scripture to us

33 In that same hour
They set out
And returned to Jerusalem
Where they found the eleven
And those who were with them
Gathered together

34 They were saying
The Lord
Has certainly been raised
And has appeared to Simon

35 Then they told them
What had happened on the road
And how they recognized him
When he broke the bread

Jesus appears to the disciples

36 As they were talking about this
He stood among them
    And said to them
        Peace be with you

37 But they were dismayed
And filled with fear
Because they supposed
That they beheld a spirit

38   He said to them
        Why are you distressed
        And why do such thoughts
        Rise up in your hearts
39   Look at my hands and my feet
        Make sure that I
        I am indeed myself
        Handle me
        Because a spirit
        Does not have flesh and bones
        As you behold that I have

40 When he had said this
He showed them
His hands and his feet

41 Overcome with joy and astonishment
They still did not believe
    So he said to them
        Have you anything to eat here?

42 And they gave him
Part of a cooked fish
And a piece of honeycomb
43 Which he took and ate
In their presence

44   And he said to them
        While I was still with you
        I told you it was necessary
        For everything to be fulfilled
        That has been written about me
        In the law of Moses
        And in the prophets and the psalms

45 Then he opened their minds
So that they understood the scripture
46   Saying to them
        This is what has been written
        The Christ must suffer
        And rise from the dead
        On the third day

47   And in his name
        There shall be proclaimed
        To all the nations
        Beginning from Jerusalem
        The need to change heart and mind
        For the forgiveness of sins

48   You are witnesses
        To all of this

49   And see
I
I send out upon you
The promise of my Father
But you should stay in the city
Until you are clothed with power
From above

The Ascension

50 Then he led them out
Almost as far as Bethany
And lifting up his hands
He blessed them

51 And it happened
That as he blessed them
He passed from them

52 They returned to Jerusalem
With great joy

53 And were always in the Temple
Praising God

References

2:23   Lev.12:2–8
3:4–6 Isa.40:3–5
4:4   Deut.8:3
4:8   Deut.6:13
4:10f Ps.91:11f
4:12 Deut.6:16
4:18f Isa.61:1f
7:27 Mal.3:1
8:10 Isa.6:9f, Jer.5:21, Ezek.12:2

10:27 Deut.6:5, Lev.19:18
13:35 Jer.22:5, Ps.118:26
18:20 Ex.20:12–16, Deut.5:16–20
19:38 Ps.118:26
19:46 Isa.56:7, Jer.7:11
20:17 Ps.118:22f
20:42 Ps.110:1
22:37 Isa.53:12